O Taste and See

O TASTE AND SEE

O Taste and See

Discovering God

Through
Imaginative Meditations

Paul W. Meier

MALCOLM CREEK
PUBLISHING
Benton, KY

O TASTE AND SEE

Copyright © 2013 by Paul W. Meier.

Published by Malcolm Creek Publishing,
Benton, KY 42025.
All rights reserved, including the right of reproduction in whole or in part in any form.

13-digit print edition ISBN: 978-0-9852850-7-4
10-digit print edition ISBN: 0-9852850-7-9

Cover Design by Mary C. Findley
Edited by Bethany F. Brengan.

Visit Paul W. Meier's website
at http://www.prayingthegospels.com

Unless noted otherwise, Scripture quotations are taken from:

NRSV: New Revised Standard Version Bible, copyright 1989, Division of Christian Education of the National Council of the Churches of Christ in the United States of America. Used by permission. All rights reserved.

Library of Congress Control Number: 2012923701

To my wife, Barbara,

and the members of St. Matthew by the Lake Lutheran Church
Benton, KY

for giving me the opportunity to study
and meditate upon the Scriptures.

O TASTE AND SEE

Table of Contents:

Introduction	...3
Story #1 John 2:1-11 Jesus Changes Water into Wine	...15
Story #2 John 2:13-22 Jesus Clears the Temple	...21
Story #3 Luke 4:38-44 Jesus Heals Many, Simon's Mother-in-law	...27
Story #4 Luke 5:12-16 The Man with Leprosy	...33
Story #5 Mark 2:1-2 Jesus Heals a Paralytic	...39
Story #6 Mark 3:7-12 Jesus Heals by the Seaside	...47
Story #7 Mark 4:35-41 Jesus Calms the Storm	...53
Story #8 Mark 5:24-34 Woman Healed of Bleeding	...59
Story #9 Mark 6:45-56 Jesus Walks on the Sea	...65
Story #10 Mark 8:22-26 Jesus Heals a Blind Man at Bethsaida	...71
Story #11 Luke 17:11-19 Ten Healed of Leprosy	...77
Story #12 Luke 7:11-17 Jesus Raises a Widow's Son	...83
Story #13 Matthew 15:21-28 Faith of a Canaanite Woman	...89
Story #14 Luke 19:1-10 Zaccheus the Tax Collector	...95
Story #15 John 8:2-11 Woman Caught in Adultery	...101
Story #16 Mark 9:14-29 Jesus Heals a Boy with an Unclean Spirit	...107
Story #17 John 4:43-53 Jesus Heals the Official's Son	...113

Story #18   Luke 9:51-62   Samarian Opposition ...121

Story #19   John 13:1-17   Jesus Washes His Disciples' Feet ...127

Story #20   Luke 2:1-17   The Birth of Jesus ...133

Story #21   Matthew 26:17-35   The Lord's Supper ...139

Story #22   Mark 14:3-9   Jesus Anointed in Bethany ...145

Story #23   Matthew 26:36-46   Jesus in Gethsemane ...151

Story #24   Matthew 26:47-56   Jesus Arrested ...157

Story #25   Mark 14:53-65   Jesus before the Sanhedrin ...163

Story #26   Matthew 27:1-2, 11-26   Jesus before Pilate ...169

Story #27   John 19:1-16   Sentenced to be Crucified ...175

Story #28   John 19:23-27   Jesus Cares for His Mother ...181

Story #29   Matthew 27:45-56   Jesus's Death ...187

Story #30   Luke 24:13-35   The Walk to Emmaus ...193

Endnotes ...198

*   *   *

*O taste and see that the L*ORD *is good;*
happy are those who take refuge in him.
Ps. 34:8

*   *   *

O TASTE AND SEE

Introduction

Jesus said, "You shall love the Lord your God with all your heart, and with all your soul, and with all your mind. This is the great and first commandment" (Matt. 22:37–38).[1]

So, has anyone ever taught you *how* to love God with all your heart?

Give me twenty-five minutes a day for the next thirty days and I'll help you fall in love with God in a pleasing and powerful way. After all, the psalmist said, "O taste and see that the Lord is good, happy are those who take refuge in him" (Ps. 34:8).

* * *

For most of my life, I found it difficult to link the God of the ancient Hebrews with *God the Father* in the New Testament. It was like trying to mix oil with water. The Old Testament God showed anger and killed people with earthquakes, floods, and poisonous snakes because of their disobedience. The Hebrew God commanded Israel to wipe out towns in the Promised Land, women and children included, so there would be no temptation to worship other gods.

Yet in the New Testament, the Creator whom Jesus called *Father* loved the world so much he sent his son so that those who trust in him will not perish but have eternal life (John 3:16). The Creator-Father that Jesus wanted to please didn't punish Pharisees, disciples, or Gentiles for their disobedience. Jesus said he was one with this Creator-Father (John 10:30), and yet Jesus never promoted the death penalty for anyone's violation of specific commandments. He said we should love our enemies, not kill them.

Mixing these conflicting images is like pouring strong coffee into Kool-Aid and telling someone, "You've got to love it." How can you love a good God/bad God with all your heart? How can you love a Deity that you fear will hurt you if you step the wrong way? I wanted an image of God that I *could* love and trust with all my heart. I wanted an image of God that drew me to God the way people who were sick and in pain were drawn to Jesus.

I found the image of the Most High I could love when I was introduced to Ignatius of Loyola's method of using the imagination to meditate on the Scriptures.

* * *

The Ancient Practice

The practice of meditation is recorded early in the Bible. Isaac went out to meditate in the field (Gen. 24:63 NKJV). David's instruction was to meditate within your heart and be still (Ps. 4:4 NKJV). There are many ways to meditate. One way involves disengaging the mind (e.g., contemplation), while another method involves the active engagement of the mind, either intellectually or imaginatively. Non-contemplatives tend to be more comfortable with the active forms of meditation, yet have had little experience with the method that uses the imagination.

Using the imagination in meditation was advanced through the experiences of Ignatius of Loyola (1491–1556) who encouraged this practice in his students. Ignatius was a Basque aristocrat and soldier. He was injured defending a town fortress on the border between Spain and France. During a lengthy recovery, he asked for reading materials. The only books available were of a religious nature. One that changed the direction of his life was the *Vita Christi* (*The Life of Christ*).

By the time Ignatius recovered enough from his wounds to walk, he decided to go to Jerusalem to live where Christ had lived. On the way, he stopped along a river at Manresa where he ended up staying ten months in a cave, spending hours in prayer each day and working in a hospice. During this time, he was blessed with visions and he received profound insights into the mysteries of the faith.

Ignatius became confident that all the things in the world are given to us so that we can know God more easily and return love more readily. He believed experiences of the presence of God were accessible to others. If the lives of ordinary people touched by the finger of God produced results like saints Augustine, Dominic, and Francis, then other ordinary people must have the same opportunity to be transformed. He developed a thirty day immersion experience called the *Spiritual Exercises*. With this, he taught people how to develop a life-changing relationship with God. I found one of the practices within the *Exercises*, meditating upon Scripture, particularly effective, and I want to teach it to you.

* * *

Because the stories of Jesus in the Gospels are Spirit-filled, they offer you and me a way to experience Jesus personally in his earthly life. One of the important daily practices in the *Spiritual Exercises* encourages participants to engage the five physical senses by imagining they are living inside the biblical stories. When I began imagining myself living within the stories and interacting with Jesus, the Bible sprang to life. Jesus became real and personal. I found out what it meant to have a "personal relationship" with a man who lived two thousand years ago. I developed feelings of affection and devotion that stirred a level of commitment greater than I had ever experienced before.

What impacted me more profoundly was taking these exercises a step further. I reflected on what Jesus said about himself and his relationship to the Father. The apostle Paul said the fullness of God is seen in Christ. Instead of simply finishing my meditation with a deeper and more committed love for Jesus, I thought, *If Jesus reveals the Father, the Creator, to us, then I should be able to transfer my increased love for Jesus to the Father by trusting that they are one with each other. Why don't I put the Father in Jesus's place and meditate upon these stories again?*

When I made the switch and imagined the Creator-Father in place of Jesus, the Holy Spirit changed my whole image and understanding of God. I had found the image of God I could love with all my heart and I began to fall in love with the Creator, loving the Lord my God with all my heart. It will work for you too, if this is your desire.

So how does inserting yourself into stories in the Bible work to do this?

* * *

Just imagine that you are walking into a peach orchard at the peak of harvest season. Luscious fruits, heavy with sweet juices, strain the branches. Imagine yourself standing under one tree. Reach up and gently grasp one of the reddish-orange peaches. Squeeze it tenderly to see if it's soft or hard. Yes, it's ripe for picking. Rotate it to see if it has any blemishes. Seeing none, break the fruit away from the branch. Lightly rub its surface to make sure it's clean. Bring the peach to your mouth and sink your teeth through its velvet skin. Feel the soft yellow flesh release a flood of juices that drip down the sides of your mouth. Lean forward so no juice drops onto your clothes. Close your eyes; chew the morsel slowly and savor the flavor.

Now, stop imagining and pay attention to something else that's taking place. Do you notice more saliva in your mouth than normal? You haven't taken a bite of a peach, yet your digestive system is responding as if you had. Your salivary glands are releasing fluids as if the experience was real. A physical reaction has been stimulated by an imagined event.

The point is this: If you can imagine an event in vivid detail, your body will respond as if it is experiencing the real thing. **You can experience God in a way similar to this that stimulates a natural response—the response of love—whether the event is real or**

imagined. Let me rephrase this and say it again: *You can experience God in a way that stimulates an innate response of love whether the event is real or imagined.* Equally important, the more physical senses you engage, the more deeply the experience will be imbedded in your consciousness. The purpose of this book is to help you learn how to use your imagination to develop a powerful image of God that kindles heartfelt love and devotion for your Creator.

* * *

"Wait a minute," you might say. "I already think God is good, and I *do* love God with all my heart." I said that for fifty years. But like most Christians, I grew up with one foot firmly planted in the Old Testament and one foot in the New Testament, blending images of God that corresponded with sixteen hundred years of church doctrine: Judge and Punisher of sin yet Merciful to repentant sinners who confessed Jesus as Lord.

Although I treasure the Old Testament and God continues to speak to me through it, studying the Old Testament doesn't insure anyone that he or she will understand the true image of God. The scribes and Pharisees were faithful men devoted to the study of Scriptures. Yet Jesus said to them on five occasions, "You do not know God" (John 7:28–29, 8:19, 8:55, 16:3, 17:25). How could they not know God? They knew those writings better than you or I ever could. Still, Jesus said, "You don't know God." Studying the writings of Moses and the prophets does not guarantee you will understand the truth about God. But then how can people love God with all their heart if they can't be certain they know God?

* * *

Before you can comprehend the depths of the Scriptures and everything they are capable of teaching you, one thing must be established in your heart and mind: *What is the nature and character of the God to whom I am asked to give my complete and total trust?* What is the truth about God?

* * *

Jesus helped me to understand the foundational character of God. Jesus reveals the Creator-Father. *The DNA of God is love.* Everything I understand about God today arises from that core trait. And Jesus is the revelation of the truth about God. Let me show you several passages from the New Testament that helped me grow confident in this claim.

No one has ever seen God. It is God the only Son. . .who has made Him known (John 1:18).

[Speaking to the Pharisees] *"You know neither me nor my Father. If you knew me, you would know my Father also"* (John 8:19).

Then Jesus cried aloud, "Whoever believes in me believes not in me but in him who sent me. And whoever sees me sees him who sent me." (John 12:44–45).

[Jesus said] *"Whoever has seen me has seen the Father"* (John 14:9b).

[Jesus] is the image of the invisible God. . .For in him all the fullness of God was pleased to dwell (Colossians 1:15, 19).

For in [Christ] the whole fullness of deity dwells bodily (Colossians 2:9).

Whoever does not love does not know God, for God is love (1 John 4:8).

* * *

There's a crucial verse in the New Testament that continues this line of thinking. John 14:6 states, *"No one comes to the Father except through me."* Yet there is another possible translation for this verse. The Greek verb *erchomai* is most often translated as "to come" but it can also be translated "to become known."[2]

John 14:6 might also be translated this way: "No one *comes to know* (comprehend, understand) the Father except through me." The strength of this interpretation is supported in the ensuing verse that confirms and completes the same line of thought:

> [Jesus said] *"I am the way, the truth, and the life. No one comes to know the Father except through me. If you know me, you will know my Father also. From now on you do know him and have seen him"* (John 14:6–7).

These verses point to a God of unlimited goodness and love. They point to a God who wants to be known, who conveyed what physical and spiritual completion looks like in a concrete, perfected form so that all could know the truth.

* * *

Jesus is the truth about God. Jesus is easy to love. Jesus inspires love for the Father Creator. Because the New Testament points to Jesus as showing us the Father Creator, Jesus is our starting point.

How Will These Meditations Help You Learn To Love God?

Richard Rohr, Franciscan priest and founder of the Center for Action and Contemplation, says, "We cannot just fall in love with abstractions but only with concrete people and concrete moments and a personal God."[3] Jesus is the concrete expression of God's being and nature. In these meditations, I will help you to imagine yourself interacting with Jesus in selected Bible stories. In some meditations, you will take on the point of view of a specific character, and in others, you will participate as guided by the narration. The more vividly you imagine a story, the more your brain will receive the episode as if you actually experienced him. You will begin to comprehend the love God has for you and you will respond the way you were designed to respond—*with feelings of love which lead to actions of love.*

Then I will help you transfer your feelings of love for Jesus into pure love for the Creator.

How to Use These Meditations

Sit in a comfortable chair with both feet on the floor. Breathe deeply and slowly for sixty seconds. Relax your muscles. Offer yourself completely to God. Begin every session with a prayer asking the Holy Spirit to guide you.

Read the text, and then read a sentence or two of my description and stop. Close your eyes and imagine yourself in the scene. Visualize objects and actions as clearly as you can. Listen for the voices of people, the sounds of animals, the rolling of wheels across hard packed earth. Touch objects. Feel their texture. Smell any odors that might be in the air. Taste the food. Watch for expressions on faces. Be open to where the Spirit guides you.

Once you've become part of the scene, move on with the story. Feel free to reflect on additional thoughts and questions that come into your mind.

The first time you imagine the story, your personal interaction with Jesus will help you to love him more. The next step will help you transfer those feelings to the One that Jesus called *Father*. Go back and imagine the story a second time with one modification. The second time you imagine it, I want you to insert a word that helps you think of the *Creator* in the place of Jesus.

*   *   *

The power of these meditations lies in this step.

*   *   *

This might be a little uncomfortable for you. It will feel like mixing the old with the new. Yet it shouldn't be a big stretch to imagine God in Jesus. Jesus said, *"The Father and I are one."* You can substitute the word *Father* for Jesus, or if that term confines you to a preconceived way of thinking, use a word like *Love* or *Goodness*. Another option is to substitute one of the broader interpretations suggested for "father" from Aramaic, *"the One from whom the breath of life comes."*[4]

Re-enter the story and experience it with your favorite option in Jesus's place. When you finish, take a moment to reflect on how this practice impacts the way you think of God.

Repetition and practice will make it easier to do this. If you have difficulty imagining a story in the same depth as others, don't give up. Take a little time to relax and let go of whatever might be distracting you. If you can't get into it one day, forgive yourself and come back the next day.

*   *   *

Although these meditations are useful for individuals in personal and private settings, retreat leaders, spiritual directors, and clergy can easily adapt them for group settings. A group setting doesn't allow participants the liberty to roam within a scene longer than is determined by the leader. Yet group discussion at the end can richly compensate in other ways. In a group setting, I encourage leaders to assume creative freedom to add to the sounds, colors, images, scents, touches, and tastes within each story.

*   *   *

Jesus used the physical senses as doorways to belief. Through seeing, speaking, feeding, and touching, the Word continues to find entry through the physical senses to bring about faith. Author and writing teacher Hal Bennett describes the five physical senses as "windows to the soul." He writes, "Words and phrases that speak to the senses...have an almost miraculous ability to narrow the distance between the writer and the reader."[5] Bennett says that stimulation of the senses awakens a deep sense of involvement that helps us cross into the life of the other.

This is my intent: to help you enter into the life of Jesus—to narrow the distance between you and the Author and Finisher of your faith (Hebrews 12:2 NKJV). My prayer is that in some way, these meditations will help you to love the Lord your God with all your heart, and with all your soul, and with all your mind.

* * *

*No one has ever seen God.
It is God the only Son,
who is close to the Father's heart,
who has made him known.*
John 1:18

* * *

Story #1   Jesus Changes Water into Wine

Weddings in Jesus's day were events of intense and passionate celebration. They represented the continuation of family, of tradition, and of a nation. They symbolized hope for the future. The whole village often took part in the celebration. Jesus compared the kingdom of God to a wedding feast. In this story, imagine that you are one of Jesus's disciples.

Take a moment to relax and then enter into the story. Pray to be led by the Holy Spirit.

See – Listen – Taste – Smell – Touch

John 2:1–11

On the third day there was a wedding in Cana of Galilee, and the mother of Jesus was there. Jesus and his disciples had also been invited to the wedding.

A villager scurries by an open doorway and shouts inside, "Jesus, don't forget, you and your disciples are invited to Judah and Rebecca's wedding. They're a fine couple, if I do say so myself. Please come!"

Jesus's eyebrows arch playfully. A party? What fun! He stands, grabs his staff and hurries out the door. You and three other disciples stumble over each other, scrambling like children getting in line for a sweet treat, trying to squeeze through the narrow doorway.

Not far away, a celebration is in full swing...aromas of roasted lamb, goat's cheese, simmering stews blend with singing and laughter. As you walk by a table, reach out and pluck a couple of fresh grapes and figs from serving plates piled high. Bite down on a grape. Its sweet juices spray into your mouth....

Bright-eyed children skip alongside the tables, running their fingers along the fringe of the table covering.

Take a moment to dance with the bride or the groom....

When the wine gave out, the mother of Jesus said to him, "They have no wine."

A wedding attendant leans over and whispers something to Judah. The groom's eyebrows lower and the furrows in his forehead deepen.

Mary notices. She leans over and whispers, "What's wrong, Judah? Is there a problem?"

He points to an empty wine carafe on a table. "We've run out. What now? How will we boost the spirits of the people to keep the celebration going?"

Mary scurries across the path and sits next to Jesus. "They're out of wine, Jesus. Do you think you can help keep the celebration going?"

And Jesus said to her, "Woman, what concern is that to you and to me? My hour has not yet come." His mother said to the servants, "Do whatever he tells you."

"Mother. Why are you worried about this? Why should I get involved in keeping this merriment going? I'm only a guest here."

Mary is not disheartened. She grabs a servant who is putting a plate of goat's meat on the banquet table. "Follow Jesus and do what he says."

Jesus strolls among the people and sees some friends from childhood. He approaches them and reminisces. "Do you remember when Rueben's old mule pulled him through the village?" They howl and ruffle Reuben's hair. Jesus scans the crowd and sees dismay on

Judah's face. His gaze drifts to the north, toward the mountain he loves....

Now standing there were six stone water jars for the Jewish rites of purification, each holding twenty or thirty gallons. Jesus said to them, "Fill the jars with water." And they filled them up to the brim. He said to them, "Now draw some out, and take it to the chief steward." So they took it.

Soon, Jesus walks up to the dear woman who lived next door when he was a child and gives her a hug. Two wedding servants trail closely behind him. He points to several large stone jars standing by a village hut and says, "Fill these with water. Then dip some out and take a sample to the wedding planner." The servants grab some buckets lying nearby and run to the well that's fifty yards away. After many trips, the stone jars begin spilling over onto the hardened dirt. The servants are breathing heavily, yet one dips a goblet into an overflowing jar and rushes it to the wedding planner....

When the steward tasted the water that had become wine, and did not know where it came from (though the servants who had drawn the water knew), the steward called the bridegroom and said to him, "Everyone serves the good wine first, and then the inferior wine after the guests have become drunk. But you have kept the good wine until now."

The steward accepts the goblet, brings it to his nostrils and delicately breathes its vapors—more for display than to nose its bouquet. Then he touches the liquid to his lips. Abruptly, he cocks his head back and looks at the cup in surprise. Pushing it toward you, he says, "Here, you taste it. I must be getting tired." You take the goblet in your hands and gently sip the new wine. The spirited nectar spreads through your mouth like warm honey. The steward sees your eyes open wide with delight and barks at Judah. "Am I imagining things, or is this new wine far superior to that which started the celebration?

Judah, you confuse us. This isn't the way it's been done before. What will people think? The best wine is usually served first. But at the same time you please us."

A look of bewilderment settles on Judah's face. "But I did nothing," he says. Quickly, he grabs a goblet and sips the new wine provided to rescue the celebration. A grin spreads across his face. He jumps to his feet and runs to his beloved to share the good news. Then he dashes to the servants and tells them, "Fill everyone's cup, quickly, quickly. Everyone must taste the new wine. Rejoice! There's an abundance for everyone and the celebration will become even better."

Jesus did this, the first of his signs, in Cana of Galilee, and revealed his glory; and his disciples believed in him.

* * *

Given that the fullness of God was shown in Jesus, visualize the story again but this time replace the name *Jesus* with a name for God that helps you imagine the Father/Creator in his place. Names to insert might be *Love*, *Goodness*, *Creator*, the *Breath of Life*, or come up with your own. Let this new encounter enrich your understanding of the nature and character of the Creator God.

When you are finished, reflect on how imagining the Creator in Jesus's place influences your understanding of God.

* * *

Jesus said,
*"If you know me, you will know my Father also.
From now on you do know him and have seen him."*
John 14:7

* * *

Story #2 Jesus Clears the Temple

The stories of Jesus cleansing the temple show him displaying an uncharacteristic emotion—anger. Let this meditation guide you in discerning how anger might fit into God's nature. Follow Jesus as you imagine this story.

Take a moment to relax. Pray to be led by the Holy Spirit, and then enter into the story.

See – Listen – Taste – Smell – Touch

John 2:13–22

The Passover of the Jews was near, and Jesus went up to Jerusalem. In the temple he found people selling cattle, sheep, and doves, and the money changers seated at their tables.

The narrow streets of Jerusalem bustle with busy vendors and excited folks from the country visiting the big city. Booths with jangling jewelry, blankets, tapestries, and more line the crowded walkways as far as the eye can see. Brightly dyed garments and fabrics hang on the walls of houses that line the street. Blankets stretched taut over wooden posts shade the vendors. Food and drink, leather goods, and medicines are spread out on tables. Coins clink in cautious exchange. Voices rise and fall as bartering reaches critical stages. A river of flowing bodies carries you through constricted passageways, like sand through an hourglass. You dodge carts and bounce off eager shoppers. Keeping up with Jesus as he makes his way through the crowd is no easy task; Jesus meets and hugs people along the way like they are his dearest friends.

A toothless old woman stands in your way. She tears a portion of bread from her pre-dawn labors and thrusts it in your face. "Child, have a taste of my freshly baked loaf...only a quadrans, only a quadrans." You reach into your coat pocket and dig out a small coin. She grins widely and shrieks with glee. Taking the loaf, you break it in half. Close your eyes and concentrate on the scent of dill wafting from its center. Share the loaf with a friend, and give a small piece to the beggar lying on the side of the pathway.

The temple courtyard is just around the corner. It will be good to feel the Presence in the temple again, to spend a little time in prayer in this holy place.

Running up to Jesus, you catch a glimpse of the temple. There's a line of people moving slowly to get into the courtyard. Stand in line with them. Greet a few people and ask where they came from. Finally, squeeze through the gate to the courtyard; you're inside.

Making a whip of cords, he drove all of them out of the temple, both the sheep and the cattle. He also poured out the coins of the money changers and overturned their tables. He told those who were selling the doves, "Take these things out of here! Stop making my Father's house a marketplace!" His disciples remembered that it was written, "Zeal for your house will consume me."

The atmosphere inside the temple courts is no different from the atmosphere outside. Chaos.

Money changes hands. People argue over rising prices. Doves coo from the colonnades. Pigeons beat their wings in fruitless flight when jostled in their wooden cages. Bawling sheep scurry away from snarling dogs. *This is holy ground?*

Dutiful participants line up to purchase animals for sacrifice. They are then herded to the appropriate doors where they give their animals...to the very people who sold them the beasts and who told them this is what they must do to satisfy the God of Abraham, Isaac, and Jacob.

A widow with her lame adult son gives her last coin to purchase a dove. A frail old woman with sun-dried cheeks and a tattered wrap trades a newly-made blanket for a coin. She, too, buys a dove for her offering.

Where is the sense of awe, reverence? Where is God in all this?

A commotion erupts within the heart of the courtyard. People scatter as if an over-stoked kiln has exploded.

Fire flares in Jesus's eyes. A whip cracks like lightning from the steps of the temple.

Jesus strikes a wooden cage with his whip, sending it crashing to the floor and liberating its wild-eyed birds. He turns over tables and sends coins and trays crashing down the temple steps. "How dare you turn my Maker's house into a two-bit flea market!"

The Jews then said to him, "What sign can you show us for doing this?" Jesus answered them, "Destroy this temple, and in three days I will raise it up." The Jews then said, "This temple has been under construction for forty-six years, and will you raise it up in three days?" But he was speaking of the temple of his body.

Priests rush to confront Jesus, their robes fluttering indignantly. "Who gives you the authority to do this? Prove that we should listen to you!"

"Destroy this temple and I will raise it again in three days. You will not stop here. You will soon sink to a much lower level in maligning the dignity and goodness of God...but I will raise this temple to new heights in three days."

"You're insane, Jesus. It took forty-six years to build this magnificent temple."

Standing there, you wonder, *Who can understand this nonconforming prophet? Will I ever understand everything about him?*

You've never seen him so upset. It never occurred to you that Jesus could get angry. Although you've seen him defeat storms on the sea, to imagine him using that power to hurt people is inconceivable. *This matter must be dear to his heart to cause such a reaction.*

Look around to assess the damage. Three tables of the money changers are upended and many coins strewn on the ground. One wooden bird cage lies slightly damaged and needing the latch on its door replaced. Several red-faced temple priests mutter their disdain. No one is physically hurt.

After he was raised from the dead, his disciples remembered that he had said this; and they believed the scripture and the word that Jesus had spoken.

The disciples recline around a table as some of the women remove serving plates. Peter says, "Make sure that door is locked."

Andrew replies, "That was the first thing I did once John got here."

"Thanks. Now, let's rehash our position. Everyone is clear that Jesus has been seen by several people. He's risen. He said it would happen, but that was too outlandish for anyone to take him seriously."

John said, "Yes, it was. But don't you remember the prophet Zechariah said, 'Do not be afraid, daughter of Zion. Look your king is coming, sitting on a donkey's colt!' That's what Jesus did!"

"Yes, and remember all the things Cleopas said Jesus explained from the scriptures as they were walking to Emmaus about how the Messiah was going to die and rise again," added James. "He openly told us that he would die and rise on the third day, but that didn't make sense at the time."

All stare into the flame of the oil lamp flickering on the table. Mary Magdalene raises her hand and cautions the women to remain still. Peter softly says, "Remember when he got upset in the temple's court of the Gentiles, how the priests were glad to take their money but wouldn't allow them into the temple itself? Who would have thought that by claiming he could rebuild the temple in three days, he was talking about his body? There's still more to that image than we've uncovered. Let's trust that what Jesus said about the Holy Spirit coming to us to help us understand all that has taken place is being fulfilled as we speak. Let us pray. . ."

* * *

Given that the fullness of God was shown in Jesus, visualize the story again but this time replace the name *Jesus* with a name for God that helps you imagine the Father/Creator in his place. Names to insert might be *Love*, *Goodness*, *Creator*, the *Breath of Life*, or come up with your own. Let this new encounter enrich your understanding of the nature and character of the Creator God.

When you are finished, reflect on how imagining the Creator in Jesus's place influences your understanding of God.

* * *

Then [the Pharisees] said to him,
"Where is your Father?"
Jesus answered, "You know neither me nor my Father.
If you knew me, you would know my Father also."
John 8:19

* * *

Story #3   Jesus Heals Many, Simon's Mother-in-Law

After teaching in the synagogue, Jesus accepted an invitation from Simon Peter to come to his home. To eat a meal with someone meant you wanted to know them and to develop a closer relationship with them. In this story, imagine yourself as Peter's mother-in-law.

Take a moment to relax. Pray to be led by the Holy Spirit, and then enter into the story.

See – Listen – Taste – Smell – Touch

Luke 4:38–44

After leaving the synagogue [Jesus] entered Simon's house. Now Simon's mother-in-law was suffering from a high fever.

"That Peter! What am I going to do with him? He gives me such short notice. He's so impulsive. I have too little time to prepare a suitable table. Yet I do enjoy entertaining, hearing news I wouldn't normally hear. And I'm flattered to host this distinguished guest in our home. The village will be pleased. . . I must hurry!"

As you scurry to remove the loaves from the oven, the normally delightful whiff of the fresh bread overpowers you. It's like the smell makes your throat close up. Then the scent of herbs in the simmering soup slaps you like high waves beating against a boat. Nausea. . .your stomach twists into a knot. You tremble, feeling like you need to put on another shawl. Chills, hot flashes. *The floor needs sweeping. They will be arriving soon.* "Oh my, I'm so light-headed. . ."

And they asked him about her. Then he stood over her and rebuked the fever, and it left her. Immediately she got up and began to serve them.

"Where am I? On my bed? What happened?" You hear voices in the next room. *The guests have arrived? I'm so embarrassed. I've got to get up. Oh, my head is spinning... All I want to do, dear God, is take care of my guests. Why is this happening to me?*

The room darkens. A man stands in the doorway.

"I don't want anyone to see me like this, Peter."

Jesus walks slowly toward you. Recognizing him, you say, "Let me get up and help you, Master." But your bed feels like it is rotating on a threshing wheel, powered by ten chariot horses. Jesus kneels at your bedside. With the gentle touch of his palm on your forehead, he tells you to be still. His hand slides from your sweaty hair to the side of your flushed face. He says, "Go away."

Gently, the whirlwind in your head fades. The knot in your stomach softens. A new vitality enters you. "Please, my Lord, I'm feeling better now...honest. Let me serve you."

Having returned to the activity, you retrieve some empty bowls from the table. It's a blessing to hear the banter of friends, some nice comments about the soup and bread. *Thank you, God, for allowing me this honor. I don't know what I'd do if I wasn't able to do this.*

> As the sun was setting, all those who had any who were sick with various kinds of diseases brought them to him; and he laid his hands on each of them and cured them. Demons also came out of many, shouting, "You are the Son of God!" But he rebuked them and would not allow them to speak, because they knew that he was the Messiah.

The meal has come to an end. The evening light slips sluggishly out the door. Yet there are a growing number of voices outside. Plates are quickly removed from the room and set to the side to be cleaned later.

A neighbor carries her little boy into the room. He has not walked since a chariot rolled over his leg two years ago. He clings to his mother like a frightened cat clinging to a tree branch. Jesus reaches for him, pulls him gently into his lap, and wraps his arms around the child. Just like any active toddler, the boy scoots off Jesus's lap and runs out the door. His mother runs after him, sobbing tears of joy.

A man enters the room clutching the side of his neck. Jesus reaches out to touch him and he leaves smiling. A woman rages at her daughter as she is led to Jesus. He lays hands on her and speaks a blessing. A new peace fills her and the two women depart laughing. It's a long but wonderful evening.

With the wavering light of an oil lamp to guide you, your bed welcomes you—no longer the spinning wheel it was a few hours earlier. Slumber is a dear friend. Tonight's rest will be as deep as your love for the Lord. A sweet peace floods over you.

At daybreak he departed and went into a deserted place. And the crowds were looking for him; and when they reached him, they wanted to prevent him from leaving them. But he said to them, "I must proclaim the good news of the kingdom of God to the other cities also; for I was sent for this purpose." So he continued proclaiming the message in the synagogues of Judea.

A rapid tapping on the door awakens you. *It's morning already?* Quickly you rise and hurry to the door. Many strangers stand impatiently outside looking for Jesus. Hope and expectation fill their eyes. "Where is Jesus?" they plead.

You answer, "His disciples told me he always rises early to find a quiet place to pray. They say he won't do without it. But I can take you to the place I told him there's a beautiful fig tree. It's beyond the ridge."

You take your time getting a wrap, and then lead a group of ten people through the village. As the tree comes into sight, Jesus walks along the ridge and speaks to you. "I'll be on my way now. Thanks so much for meal and attentive service last evening."

The crowd laments, "Stay with us, Jesus. Who will help us if you're not here?"

Jesus responds, "There are many hands to serve right here. But you know where to find me if something goes wrong. I must keep travelling to tell others the blessings that come when they allow God to reign in their lives. This is why I was sent. More people need to hear of the Creator's goodness."

* * *

Given that the fullness of God was shown in Jesus, visualize the story again but this time replace the name *Jesus* with a name for God that helps you imagine the Father/Creator in his place. Names to insert might be *Love*, *Goodness*, *Creator*, the *Breath of Life*, or come up with your own. Let this new encounter enrich your understanding of the nature and character of the Creator God.

When you are finished, reflect on how imagining the Creator in Jesus's place influences your understanding of God.

* * *

*Whoever does not love
does not know God,
for God is love.*
1 John 4:8

* * *

Story #4   The Man with Leprosy

Leprosy is a disease that deadens the nerve endings in the skin. Lepers lose their sense of touch. Because they cannot feel pain, they don't know when damage is being done to their skin by fire, sharp objects, etc. In biblical days, this condition rendered people social outcasts, unclean. Leprosy was considered a punishment from God. Become the leper in today's meditation.

Take a moment to relax. Pray to be led by the Holy Spirit, and then enter into the story.

See – Listen – Taste – Smell – Touch

Luke 5:12–16

Once, when [Jesus] was in one of the cities, there was a man covered with leprosy.

Yesterday, you were fortunate enough to meet two other lepers who shared their meal with you. You tried to be of assistance by removing the pan from the fire. After they spooned out some soup, a putrid odor mixed with the flavor of the broth. You looked down. Smoke was coming from your hand, still holding the pan handle. That's when you realized it was your skin burning.

When you woke up today, your palm was blistered, draining blood and pus. You found a clean wrap to cover it, but it contaminates quickly. Every few hours you unwind the soiled rag, rinse it in some water from the well, and rewrap it. You've got other cuts and bruises, but you don't know where half of them came from. You have no way of replacing damaged or torn clothing. No one will let you work for them. They say you're unclean. That God has cursed you with this disorder. Even the religious spit at you. *I know I'm not perfect but the*

Almighty who made the beauty I've seen can't be as vindictive as they think. I'm not dirt. I can't imagine anything I did that would bring this kind of punishment. Yet you hear a new rabbi is in the village who is a healer. . .

> When he saw Jesus, he bowed with his face to the ground and begged him, "Lord, if you choose, you can make me clean."

You're afraid to approach another "man of God." All they seem to do is insult and condemn you, but you've heard this one is compassionate. What do you have to lose? Here he comes. . .

Dropping to the ground, desperation merges with the dust clinging to your fingers. Tears, stored during months of isolation, run down your cheeks. "Lord, I don't know why I'm like this. I'm sorry if I did anything to bring it on myself. I've heard you helped others, so I know you have the ability to help me. Please, if you choose, you can make me clean."

> Then Jesus stretched out his hand, touched him, and said, "I do choose. Be made clean." Immediately the leprosy left him.

The sound of his voice is like sweet music, and the words he speaks lift a weight from your spirit. You aren't sure if anything has happened, but as you raise your head from the ground, the soft warmth of a human hand slides from the back of your head along your ear and rests, cupping your cheek in his palm. You haven't felt the caress of a human hand for months.

Instinctively, you clutch his hand with your bandaged hand and direct it across your eyes and nose.

Open your eyes to see Jesus on his knees in front of you. He places his other hand on your other cheek and holds your face in his hands. Let his eyes speak to you.

And [Jesus] ordered him to tell no one. "Go," he said, "and show yourself to the priest, and, as Moses commanded, make an offering for your cleansing, for a testimony to them."

"Anything you say, Lord." You wrap your arms around him, embarrassed that you might be dirtying his tunic, then turn and leave. *How can I not tell anyone? This is the best day of my life! To feel the touch of another's hand again. . . And my burned palm, ouch, it hurts! But it's good!* It's clean. A new layer of skin is forming. Now you will know when you've done something to hurt yourself and avoid it. You never thought pain would feel so good.

You lean down and pull a small rock from your sandal. *I would not have felt that if I were not healed. By nightfall, it would have opened another wound. Why shouldn't I tell others how he changed my life? Doesn't he want people to know he's not like the other religious leaders? He helps outcasts. He doesn't condemn them. I'll try to keep this to myself, but people are going to ask me, "What's happened to you?" I don't know what I can tell them but the truth.*

Picking up speed, you hurry to the priests and show them you're no longer unclean. "As soon as I collect my possessions and get back to my house, I will bring a thank offering as Moses has prescribed." *I will surely give an offering of thanksgiving—every day of my life!—and all people will know I am committed to my God.*

But now more than ever the word about Jesus spread abroad; many crowds would gather to hear him and to be cured of their diseases. But he would withdraw to deserted places and pray.

After talking to the priests, you dash to the edge of the village to collect your meager belongings. All you say to your leper friends when you hold up your unwrapped hand is, "There's someone you need to talk to. His name is Jesus, and I'm going home!" Everyone in the village is stirred up. The priests are asking questions. "How did

Thomas the leper get well? He wouldn't tell us what happened. He said something about a new rabbi. What's going on?"

The next day, you hear that Jesus has been in a village three kilometers away. He stayed for several hours and then left. *He's a mystery, coming in like the wind and going out again...*

* * *

Given that the fullness of God was shown in Jesus, visualize the story again but this time replace the name *Jesus* with a name for God that helps you imagine the Father/Creator in his place. Names to insert might be *Love*, *Goodness*, *Creator*, the *Breath of Life*, or come up with your own. Let this new encounter enrich your understanding of the nature and character of the Creator God.

When you are finished, reflect on how imagining the Creator in Jesus's place influences your understanding of God.

* * *

Jesus said,
"The Father and I are one."
John 10:30

* * *

Story #5 Jesus Heals a Paralytic

Paralysis is the inability to move a portion of the body, mind, or spirit in usual manner. The causes of paralysis are many: fear, grief, ignorance, etc., as well as physical damage to an organ or limb. Before you begin this meditation, think about anything in your mind, body, or spirit that slows your movement forward in life. Imagine yourself as the one who is paralyzed.

Take a moment to relax. Pray to be led by the Holy Spirit, and then enter into the story.

See – Listen – Taste – Smell – Touch

Mark 2:1–12

When [Jesus] returned to Capernaum after some days, it was reported that he was at home. So many gathered around that there was no longer room for them, not even in front of the door; and he was speaking the word to them.

"What day is today?" you ask your neighbor, John, propping yourself up on an elbow. He sets a bowl of hot broth on a flat rock. "If I didn't know any better, I'd say it's the same day it was yesterday. . .and the day before."

He says, "Eat this. We're going to leave soon to run some errands in Capernaum today."

You say, "Okay, I'll go along. That will give me something to do." As usual, you start complaining, "I'm tired of staying in one place all the time. I'm no further ahead today than I was last year. Everyone else seems to be making progress. They're getting ahead while I feel stuck. Who wants or needs half a person? I'm just in the way. I've lost any skills I used to have; everything is an effort."

John tightens a cord on the crude tent constructed for you after your accident. He says, "Jeremiah and Dan are going with us, too. Where are your mat poles? By the way, did you hear Jesus is in town again?"

"Why are people so excited that he's back? Everyone was jabbering about him at the evening meal. I don't know why they get so animated. They told me they've seen him heal people; I don't believe it. They say he's from God. He can go back for all I care. God can't be real. If there was a God, I wouldn't be paralyzed like this."

Then some people came, bringing to him a paralyzed man, carried by four of them.

John says, "As a matter of fact, that's one of the stops we're going to make. We heard Jesus is going to be home until the marketplace closes."

"Oh, no...you're not going to take me to him. I don't want you to pull me into that group of hypocrites—they think they're better than everyone else. Besides, I haven't cleaned up yet. My back hurts when you carry me on that mat. I haven't eaten. I wanted to finish the basket I was weaving last week...or last month. I don't want you to do this. I hate it when people don't let me do what I want to do. I want to crawl in a hole and die."

And when they could not bring him to Jesus because of the crowd, they removed the roof above him; and after having dug through it, they let down the mat on which the paralytic lay.

Jeremiah, Eli, and Dan walk up to your tent and greet John with a hug and a slap on his back. Your mat is woven with strips of dried aquatic grass; they slide two stout walking sticks into the two sleeves on each side of the mate so you can be carried. A wool blanket softens the surface of the mat as your friends lift you from the ground. Ignoring your complaints, they set out for the house where Jesus is teaching.

"Hey, be careful," you whimper. "I almost slid off this thing." You watch with disgust as many people, like brain-washed idiots, wide-eyed, run ahead of you.

After making several exchanges during the trip, your friends finally stop and set you down in front of Jesus's home. People, mostly healthy, stand three deep and blocking the doorway.

No one moves to let you in. They don't care about you and your problems. They only care about their needs. . .and the rules they want everyone to follow but don't follow themselves. They're so tight with each other that outsiders can't break in. There's no way to get inside. *Thank heavens.* "We can't get in, fellas. Let's go on to the next errand."

Jeremiah has an idea. He points to the stairs on the side of the house. Tightly you grip the top of the mat for fear of tumbling off, they ascend the steps to the roof. "Stop, you're going to make me fall!" They laugh and ignore the irritation in your voice. It's a flat roof, usually a good place to spend the evening while the rooms cool for the night. Your friends know there's always a way to get into the house from the rooftop. One searches for a ceiling latch while the others find some rope on the roof and begin to tie it to the poles supporting the mat.

I might as well give up; there's no sense in fighting what I can't control. I'll have to submit to the mortification of being put on display in front of all those religious fanatics. You anticipate hearing them tell you that you don't have enough faith when they see nothing about your condition is going to change. Grudgingly, you grip the sides of the mat as they slowly lower you into the room.

As you reach the floor, all eyes are locked on you. Jesus, too, is looking at you. You've never felt as much like a target as you do now.

But Jesus's gaze is different; it's like he's looking through you, like he sees the cause of your paralysis. Your soul lies naked and there's nowhere to hide. . . . He sees that you don't believe he can help you. Nothing could be more humiliating than to have your weakness paraded in front of these hypocrites. You cry in your heart, "Dear God, help me!"

When Jesus saw their faith, he said to the paralytic, "Son, your sins are forgiven."

Jesus turns his head upward. He sees your friends who lowered you on the mat. He smiles like a father who is proud of his children. You wait for him to tell you the same things you've heard from most religious people. They say you are to blame for your condition.

But Jesus doesn't browbeat you with a sermon. He doesn't tell you that you have to do something to help yourself. He says, "Your sins are forgiven." A heaviness dissipates. You don't know what he means. *I'm forgiven? A lot of good that does me. Isn't he going to tell me how to fix my life?*

Now some of the scribes were sitting there, questioning in their hearts, "Why does this fellow speak in this way? It is blasphemy! Who can forgive sins but God alone?" At once Jesus perceived in his spirit that they were discussing these questions among themselves;

Those teachers of the law in their ceremonial robes. . . Their self-serving piety repulses you. And how can Jesus forgive you when you can't even forgive yourself? You had taken your father's donkey out for a ride over rough terrain without permission. It stepped in a hole, breaking a leg and throwing you to the ground. You haven't been able to move your legs since that incident.

Your dad couldn't afford another donkey and had no way of bringing lumber to the city anymore. He got so depressed. Things were never the same... *It was my fault.*

...and he said to them, "Why do you raise such questions in your hearts? Which is easier, to say to the paralytic, 'Your sins are forgiven,' or to say, 'Stand up and take your mat and walk'? But so that you may know that the Son of Man has authority on earth to forgive sins"—he said to the paralytic—"I say to you, stand up, take your mat and go to your home."
And he stood up, and immediately took the mat and went out before all of them; so that they were all amazed and glorified God, saying, "We have never seen anything like this!"

Still caught up in your own internal dialogue, you hear Jesus tell you to get up and go home. "What? 'Carry my mat out of here?' My pleasure. There's nothing I'd like better than to get out of here." Without thinking, you roll off the edge of your mat and push yourself up to sit on your haunches. Rolling one side pole toward the other, the mat spools around it until it reaches the opposite pole. Using them to steady yourself, you place one foot solidly on the ground, reach higher on the poles and pull yourself up. Beads of sweat form on your brow. Then you take a step toward the doorway and the poles come to a horizontal position at your side. Wide-eyed, people begin to move to the side.

"Get out of my way," you scowl. The room is small and you reach the door quickly. As you walk through the doorway, you think, *That was easier than I expected walking through all those people.* The crunch of gravel under your sandals reaches your ears.

Wait a minute! Gravel is crunching under MY sandals? And I'm outside the house? "Oh, my God! I'm walking! I'm walking! Where are my friends?"

You turn and look back into the house. The people don't appear as menacing...or as self-righteous as you made them out to be. Many of them are smiling and clapping, rejoicing to see you moving forward again. Praise God!

* * *

Given that the fullness of God was shown in Jesus, visualize the story again but this time replace the name *Jesus* with a name for God that helps you imagine the Father/Creator in his place. Names to insert might be *Love, Goodness, Creator*, the *Breath of Life*, or come up with your own. Let this new encounter enrich your understanding of the nature and character of the Creator God.

When you are finished, reflect on how imagining the Creator in Jesus's place influences your understanding of God.

* * *

*Then Jesus cried aloud:
"Whoever believes in me
believes not in me
but in him who sent me.
And whoever sees me
sees him who sent me."*
John 12:44-45

* * *

Story #6   Jesus Healing by the Seaside

Jesus's reputation has spread all over Israel. People are telling their family and friends what they have seen and experienced through his healings, touchings, and power over evil spirits. Expectations are high. People push forward. Their belief that he can help them with specific problems inspires them to seek him with all their strength.

In this story, imagine yourself as someone in the back of the crowd. You are sick, weak, and diseased. How much do you want to be healed? What do you hope for once you reach Jesus? What is your deepest need?

Take a moment to relax. Pray to be led by the Holy Spirit, and then enter into the story.

See – Listen – Taste – Smell – Touch

Mark 3:7–12

Jesus departed [from the synagogue] with his disciples to the sea, and a great multitude from Galilee followed him; hearing all that he was doing, they came to him in great numbers from Judea, Jerusalem, Idumea, beyond the Jordan, and the region around Tyre and Sidon.

Standing on the shoreline, look out at the sea. Take a deep breath and feel a strong breeze sweep past your cheeks. Something about this large expanse of water calms the spirit. Gaze out upon the water and behold the vastness of God's goodness and love. It speaks the unfathomable mystery of life. Many are drawn to the water, to rest, to be filled.

A friend told you that Jesus of Nazareth—healer, teacher extraordinaire, exorcist—is near the lake. People have said he healed them. Could you ever be that lucky?

You've tried everything: herbs, potions, rituals, incantations, fasting. Your pain has only increased. The sea has been the only place to find some peace, some grace.

I will walk as far as I must to find him. Jesus isn't difficult to find—all one has to do is follow everyone else who is blind, lame, sick, or mentally unstable.

Slowly getting to your feet, join the crowd. It takes so much effort. You can't walk as fast as others. People join in behind you. "Stop pushing me," you say to the people pressing against you. They want to see him. *I want to see him too.* Press against the woman ahead of you. Nudge her to get her to move ahead. So many of these people are not even able to care for their basic needs, wandering in the stench of human despair. The body odor and smell of urine is rank. Listen as the strangers around you talk to each other about their fears, their hopes. Will there be enough healing to go around? Will Jesus stay long enough for us to reach the front of the line?

Some who are behind you push their way past you to get to Jesus. They have good feet and legs. "Hey, wait! I'm at a disadvantage even here." A bolt of pain shoots through your hip. It takes your breath away. *I don't know if I can do this. . .* You watch others ahead of you meet Jesus. They leave, healed. Others say, "That's not fair. Isn't Jesus supposed to heal in the order that we get in line? Don't they care about our needs?"

Do those people know an easier way to get to him? They wait for a small opening and they slip through the crowd easily. Remind yourself not to let your anger or frustration become greater than your desire to be healed. Be patient. You don't have the strength to fight your way through the masses. Besides, if healing has anything to do with your own strength, you'll be disappointed again.

He told his disciples to have a boat ready for him because of the crowd, so that they would not crush him; for he had cured many, so that all who had diseases pressed upon him to touch him. Whenever the unclean spirits saw him, they fell down before him and shouted, "You are the Son of God!" But he sternly ordered them not to make him known.

The crowd inches ahead ever so slowly. Pay attention to the others. There's a man who is blind. How awful it must be to not be able to see. He can't find his way to Jesus on his own. He's not forcing his way through the crowd. He's getting closer the only way he knows how... He simply moves along with the rest of you. The elderly woman next to you uses a crutch because she's paralyzed on one side from a stroke. She can't move any faster than a step at a time. If the crowd was moving any faster, she'd be knocked off her feet and trampled.

As you get closer to Jesus, the crowd diverts around a man passed out in his own vomit. The smell turns your stomach. Many walk around him. Amazingly, two brothers reach down to lift him up; they stand on each side of him and support him. Even though there's a lot of pushing and shoving, the crowd seems to be holding everyone up.

You're inching ever closer to Jesus... You are almost there. Someone actually laughs. A few eyes betray hope.

Jesus stands by the boat. He puts his hands on each person as they come near. The blind man who walked with you kneels at Jesus' feet. He bends down, lightly touches the man's eyes and kisses his head. The man gasps as he stands, tears stream down his cheeks. "Thank you, Jesus," he cries and walks briskly away seeing all things clearly. The woman paralyzed on one side explains her problem. Jesus smiles and touches her side. Grinning and holding her crutch above her head, she skips away with new direction and strength. Even the man who had passed out and was covered in his own vomit walks away cleansed, a man with a fresh start.

Oh, Jesus. . .I'm next. Kneeling before him, you're speechless. Jesus smiles. He reaches forward and touches you. . .and the deepest ache in your soul is gone, an ocean of peace spills into your inner being.

* * *

Given that the fullness of God was shown in Jesus, visualize the story again but this time replace the name *Jesus* with a name for God that helps you imagine the Father/Creator in his place. Names to insert might be *Love*, *Goodness*, *Creator*, the *Breath of Life*, or come up with your own. Let this new encounter enrich your understanding of the nature and character of the Creator God.

When you are finished, reflect on how imagining the Creator in Jesus's place influences your understanding of God.

* * *

Jesus said,
*"Very truly, I tell you,
the Son can do nothing on his own,
but only what he sees the Father doing;
for whatever the Father does,
the Son does likewise."*
John 5:19

* * *

Story #7   Jesus Calms the Storm

The Sea of Galilee is susceptible to sudden, violent storms. Powerful winds can sweep through the mountain passes and descend on the lake without warning. As you meditate on this story, try to relate the experience of the physical storm to a personal disruption in your life such as a divorce, a death, a defeat in school or your career, an unexpected job transfer, a major change in your health, etc., especially if the disruption came unexpectedly. Imagine yourself in a small fishing boat twenty-five to thirty feet long with five or six people.

Take a moment to relax. Pray to be led by the Holy Spirit, and then enter into the story.

See – Listen – Taste – Smell – Touch

Mark 4:35–41

On that day, when evening had come, [Jesus] said to them, "Let us go across to the other side." And leaving the crowd behind, they took him with them in the boat, just as he was. Other boats were with him.

Standing knee deep in water, you've been holding the boat steady for Jesus. The sun has been hot and the water feels refreshing. Many people came to hear Jesus teach. They crowded so close to him that he stepped into a fishing boat. You held the boat so it wouldn't drift away or rock when he shifted his weight. You are grateful he takes the time to explain the meaning of his parables. Some of his stories contain as much mystery as they do practical application.

Jesus suggests getting away from the crowd. You and the rest of the disciples gladly welcome the break.

A breeze blows across the water; it will only take an hour to get to the other side of the lake. You tell everyone, "Get into the boat" and start pushing the boat away from the shore. Your feet spray water against the side of the boat and you get ready to jump into the boat. Oh, no... The boat slips freely into deeper water. You try to grab onto the edge, but the boat glides away more quickly than expected, and you're left hanging onto the side, holding on for dear life. Your friends double over in laughter and then pull you into the boat by your arms. Red-faced, you wring out your loose clothing.

A great windstorm arose, and the waves beat into the boat, so that the boat was already being swamped.

After only twenty minutes of sailing, dark billowing clouds appear and the sky rumbles like a hundred chariots are passing overhead. The temperature of the wind drops. Someone shouts at you to lower the sail. An angry wind whips the sturdy fabric like it's a leaf. The heavens throw darts of lightning at your boat. You're too far from shore to turn back. Whitecaps crash against the boat as it bobs in waves five feet high. Sheets of piercing raindrops sting your face.

Trying to keep the boat stable, you grab a set of oars. "Hey, Peter! Keep the nose of the boat pointed forward!"

Ouch. You taste blood. A wild rope must have swung free and busted your lip. Blisters, from gripping the oars, break open on your hands. Peter and James are shouting orders. Water crashes onto the floor of the boat. "Help us, God of Abraham! Where is Jesus? Has anybody seen him?"

But he was in the stern, asleep on the cushion; and they woke him up and said to him, "Teacher, do you not care that we are perishing?" He woke up and rebuked the wind, and said to the sea, "Peace! Be still!"

"What? He's asleep in the back of the boat? Doesn't he know we need help?" Angrily, you stagger to your feet, tripping as you step over Peter. A wave hits the side, knocking you to your knees. A sharp pain shoots through your wrist as you cushion your fall. Your shins will soon reveal bruises. Your fear and anger match the intensity of the storm. "Jesus!"

He lies sleeping propped between two small barrels packed with fishing nets. A piece of hardened sail cloth shields him from the rain. How amazingly peaceful he looks. Is he so tired that he doesn't realize the danger? "Jesus! Why aren't you helping us?! We're going to die and you don't even care!"

Jesus wakes. He looks at the storm. Then his eyes meet yours. (*Stop here and meditate on what Jesus' eyes say to you. . .*)

Standing, he turns and looks into the raging storm's heart and says, "Quiet, be still."

Then the wind ceased, and there was a dead calm. He said to them, "Why are you afraid? Have you still no faith?"

As you stand there trying to catch your breath, the wind begins to whimper. The waves roll softly to stillness. Raising your head, the sun's last rays fall into the night and the hammering clouds of trouble dissipate like feathers in the sky. You look around and see other boats on the water. It appears they made it through too. You wave and shout to them, "Are you okay? Is everyone all right?"

Turning to Jesus, you say, "Thanks, Jesus." Jesus returns to his resting place and sits down, and his eyes meet yours again. . . (*What do they say to you now?*)

And they were filled with great awe and said to one another, "Who then is this, that even the wind and the sea obey him?"

How can this be? One moment, the sky is falling and every element in nature is opposing you, and the next, the sea has become like glass. Jesus had no fear. He simply told it all to stop. How can he do that? He's like no other teacher. . . like no other man. Who has power over the wind?

* * *

Given that the fullness of God was shown in Jesus, visualize the story again but this time replace the name *Jesus* with a name for God that helps you imagine the Father/Creator in his place. Names to insert might be *Love, Goodness, Creator*, the *Breath of Life*, or come up with your own. Let this new encounter enrich your understanding of the nature and character of the Creator God.

When you are finished, reflect on how imagining the Creator in Jesus's place influences your understanding of God.

* * *

Jesus said to him,
"Have I been with you all this time, Philip,
and you still do not know me?
Whoever has seen me
has seen the Father."
John 14:9

* * *

Story #8 Woman Healed of Bleeding

Today's story occurs as Jesus is on his way to help the dying daughter of a synagogue leader. The crowd expects that another miracle is imminent. Many want to witness a miracle so that they can see for themselves and believe in him. Yet they fail to notice a miracle as it occurs in their presence. Imagine yourself as the woman who desires to be made whole. Imagine what she thinks as she fights her way to get closer to Jesus.

Take a moment to relax. Pray to be led by the Holy Spirit, and then enter into the story.

See – Listen – Taste – Smell – Touch

Mark 5:24–34

So [Jesus] went with [Jairus, whose daughter was ill].
And a large crowd followed him and pressed in on him. Now there was a woman who had been suffering from hemorrhages for twelve years. She had endured much under many physicians, and had spent all that she had; and she was no better, but rather grew worse.

Will I ever get over this? You are so weary of this bleeding that has persisted for twelve years. You paid a fortune trying to identify a cause. No medical professional was able to discover the origin of your disorder. Others know you have a problem. It's not easy to hide chronic blood loss that seeps through clothing. Blood flow, as a bodily discharge, makes you ceremonially unclean. People stare at you with suspicion. Their eyes question, "Why is God doing that to you?" As the blood drains, life-giving energy goes with it. It's hard to motivate yourself. You can't even muster the interest do the things you used to enjoy doing. Every day is like trudging through a thick, muddy pit only to get to the next day. *What can I do to recover my life?*

She had heard about Jesus, and came up behind him in the crowd and touched his cloak, for she said, "If I but touch his clothes, I will be made well." Immediately her hemorrhage stopped; and she felt in her body that she was healed of her disease.

Religious leaders tell you God is punishing you because of some terrible sin you committed. They have no idea what is causing your problem either, but it's an answer that absolves them of their inability to help. You wonder, "Why would God be so malicious, making me suffer for something I don't even know I've done? Is God mad at me for being a woman?"

A friend encourages you saying, "The rabbi, Jesus, has healed people with greater problems than yours." Your eyes light up. *If others with greater problems have been healed, I know he can make my chronic condition go away.*

But you don't want to be the center of attention. For twelve years you've covered your face in public, trying to be invisible. Why attract anyone's attention? If you can just sneak up to him and touch him, he might help you without anyone noticing. You just have to get to him.

People are packed like hungry sheep on the narrow, dirt street. They crowd around him. You can't break through the mass of people. You have kept to yourself for so long; it's uncomfortable touching and being touched by others. Getting among all these excited people who are so determined to keep their eyes on Jesus makes you terribly anxious. They push you one way and then another. But you are determined, *I won't let them decide my success or failure, or even the direction I go. I must reach him. I have no other hope...*

Push your way through the mass of people. Some smell bad. Some sound sick. Some are simply bystanders. A meek attempt will not suffice. Summon the determination, turn sideways, and press between two onlookers. They're only observing and won't care if you pass them by. Others are so intent on getting to him, they don't notice you. You don't fault them for trying get closer to him too. *Their needs are no less than my own.*

Yet I feel invisible in this sea of people. They see me but they don't. But how can they know the internal problem that I have never shared with them? Their mouths move in greeting, but I hear nothing. They might be good people. And maybe they care for me as much as I care for them.

Maybe if I walk among them, the momentum of our efforts together will move me closer to him. Slide a little closer to Jesus when the person in front of you turns to look back. You're getting very close, within arm's length. *But I'm not important enough to confront him directly.* Especially in front of all these people. Almost there. . .

Now stretch out with your hand—stretch a little more and touch his clothes. There. . . There. *I've touched his robe. Oh! Oh my! It's true. It's true.* Simply touching his robe. . . just like that! And your burden is let go. "Oh, praise be to the God of Abraham!" You are healed and you can feel it; a new energy is released into the depths of your soul. "Praise God!"

Did anyone notice? No. *Good, I want to fade into the crowd so I can go on home. . .and rejoice in my healing. Praise God*

Immediately aware that power had gone forth from him, Jesus turned about in the crowd and said, "Who touched my clothes?" And his disciples said to him, "You see the crowd pressing in on you; how can you say, 'Who touched me?'" He looked all around to see who had done it. But the woman, knowing what had happened to her, came in fear and trembling, fell down before him, and told him the whole truth.

But wait. Oh no. Jesus is now calling for you. *Does he want to make a spectacle of me? I don't want anybody's attention. The law says women aren't supposed to be so bold with men in public. And I'm unclean. I'm not supposed to be among people without being cleansed. I don't want him to chastise me for wanting to be whole.*

Falling on your knees, you speak. "Rabbi, forgive me. I was afraid of you. I didn't feel worthy of your attention. My children pay no attention to me anymore. I lost my purpose for living. My life was draining away and I needed help. You were my only hope. And because I reached out to you, I have felt your goodness instead of your wrath, even though I have sinned. Please let me go home. There are some important things I must do."

He said to her, "Daughter, your faith has made you well; go in peace, and be healed of your disease."

"Daughter? You call me daughter?" Another weight lifts from your heart. You speak with more freedom and courage, "I'm so relieved you are not angry with me, Rabbi. I've only wanted to please God. I've done the work of three men to try to make up for my shortcomings. Now I know the truth about the God you speak of who loves me in spite of what others say about me.

"Maybe others have the same problem I did, and they'll see how reaching out to touch your robe can help them too. You changed my life. I'm healed. Thank you, Jesus."

* * *

Given that the fullness of God was shown in Jesus, visualize the story again but this time replace the name *Jesus* with a name for God that helps you imagine the Father/Creator in his place. Names to insert might be *Love*,

Goodness, *Creator*, the *Breath of Life*, or come up with your own. Let this new encounter enrich your understanding of the nature and character of the Creator God.

When you are finished, reflect on how imagining the Creator in Jesus's place influences your understanding of God.

* * *

Jesus said,
*"But they will do all these things to you
on account of my name,
because they do not know him who sent me."*
John 15:21 (NKJV)

* * *

Story #9   Jesus Walks on the Sea

In both the Gospels of Matthew and John, the story of Jesus walking on the sea follows the story where he began with a small amount of food and fed thousands of people. The disciples must have felt overwhelmed and tired as they collected the leftover bread into baskets. Yet instead of finding a place to settle down for the night, Jesus sends his disciples to a city across the lake. He himself must have been tired as well as surprised with what God had been doing through him. Now Jesus wants a little time alone to pray.

Take a moment to relax. Pray to be led by the Holy Spirit, and then enter into the story.

See – Listen – Taste – Smell – Touch

Mark 6:45–56

Immediately [Jesus] made his disciples get into the boat and go on ahead to the other side, to Bethsaida, while he dismissed the crowd. After saying farewell to them, he went up on the mountain to pray.

You and the other disciples finish picking up leftover bread that remains from feeding a multitude. There's so much more food to share after Jesus has revealed his power. One blessing just leads to another. With your basket full of collected bread, you ask a group that was sitting together, "Do you mind taking this to one of the villages nearby? I'm sure there are others who are hungry and would benefit. I've got some other things my Lord has asked me to do." With a warm embrace, they take it, smile, and wish you well.

"Hey, James, untie the boat, and let's get started across the lake."

Jesus told you to go ahead and prepare the next city to receive him. Does the work never end? Obediently, you and James put your weight against the boat to slide it from its muddy mooring, and then splashing through the cool water, you climb over the edge of the boat.

Inside the boat, you find a bench and sit down to catch your breath. The last rays of light drain from the sky, and you calculate when you'll be able to rest for the night. Yet James begins to talk about the people he helped to feed that day. John tells a story of his experience. They say to you, "How many people did you give bread to?"

Before you can answer, Bartholomew chimes in, "You know the prophets tell us it is God's will that we feed the poor."

James replies, "Yes, but one proverb says a slack hand causes poverty."

Lightning flashes in Bartholomew's eyes. Andrew doesn't notice and begins telling his story of feeding the people.

Jesus stayed behind to spend some time in prayer. His absence in the boat is more conspicuous as the tension increases. You wish you had more time to relax and renew. Someday you'll have the time. But right now you have too much to do to prepare the way for Jesus.

When evening came, the boat was out on the sea, and [Jesus] was alone on the land. When he saw that they were straining at the oars against an adverse wind, he came towards them early in the morning, walking on the sea. He intended to pass them by.

The stories of ministry dwindle. The halfhearted work of rowing across the lake continues until a menacing wind out of the northeast begins resisting your efforts. The effort increases while the forward progress decreases. Andrew encourages your group, "We've faced storms before, friends. We'll overcome it." Experience has taught you several ways to position the boat to make headway, and everyone has an opinion about the best approach in this circumstance. Some like to use the wind to their advantage, using its energy to fill the sails. But that's an indirect approach and the long way around. Others demand you meet the opponent head-on. It's more work and requires you to keep your hands on the oars. It spawns more blisters, and you have to be ready to respond to any sudden and powerful thrust of the foe.

This storm grows more persistent and vicious. The sky that was mildly irritable is now angry. Lightning streaks through the heavens and reveals thunderclouds churning like molten mountains. A blinding flash cracks dangerously close; sharp beads of hail sting your skin, and the sea opens its mouth as if to swallow you.

Peter shouts at James to push the barrels holding old fishing nets over the side of the boat: "We'll find them in the morning." Sweat, rain, and lake water invade every stitch of fabric, adding weight to the exhaustion already pulling you down. You're only halfway to your goal of crossing the lake; white caps smash against the boat, and you lurch forward, emptying your stomach of its meager contents. A blast of wind and water slaps the boat sideways.

"Don't stop rowing. We're losing more ground than we're gaining. I wish Jesus was here! We could use another man at the oars."

> *But when they saw him walking on the sea, they thought it was a ghost and cried out; for they all saw him and were terrified. But immediately he spoke to them and said, "Take heart, it is I; do not be afraid."*

A faint figure comes into view through the torrent. It's the shape of a man. He appears to be walking on the roiling water. *What is that? Why does he not sink into the deep? No one can do that.*

"Hey, people! Row harder!" The mission is in danger. What more could happen to destroy your efforts? *Is an evil spirit coming to sabotage what we are trying to accomplish for Jesus?* Ice pellets again prick the skin of your neck as you strain at the oars.

"Just row harder!" you shout.

But others in the boat are sidetracked. They've abandoned their rowing. "What is that on the water?" "Will it destroy us?" "God of Abraham, save us!"

The threatening hallucination speaks, "It's me. Don't be afraid."

Then he got into the boat with them and the wind ceased. And they were utterly astounded, for they did not understand about the loaves, but their hearts were hardened.

Jesus! How did he get out here in the middle of the sea? Reaching out to him, you grab one of his arms while Bartholomew grabs the other. He steps over the side and into the wind-tossed boat. And the rolling waves diminish. The boat sways gently, the clouds slide away, and the surface of the lake softens.

Totally confused, Andrew says, "Jesus, what were you doing out here? You could have been hurt with all this lightning!"

Peter says, "It's a lucky thing we ran into you. You could have drowned. We're always saving you from the trouble you get yourself into. We did that earlier today. If you hadn't had us to give out the loaves and fishes, you'd never have been able to serve all those people. You certainly do some strange things, Jesus. I've never seen anyone go for a stroll in the middle of a tempest. And *that* was a mighty big tempest!"

When they had crossed over, they came to land at Gennesaret and moored the boat. When they got out of the boat, people at once recognized him, and rushed about that whole region and began to bring the sick on mats to wherever they heard he was.

And wherever he went, into villages or cities or farms, they laid the sick in the marketplaces, and begged him that they might touch even the fringe of his cloak; and all who touched it were healed.

Upon reaching the land, you jump into the shallow water and tie the boat to a post. Jesus steps out of the boat and people come running to him. You haven't even had time to prepare the way for him. The word has spread. "Jesus helps the sick. He turns no one away. He doesn't care that the religious leaders condemn and blame people for their sickness."

You can't go anywhere without hordes of peasants bringing their family members with every kind of problem to him. Some of them are disgusting. And some aren't even your people.

He stops for each person who bow lows to the ground and touches the fringe around the bottom of his cloak. He smiles and lays his hands on them. They walk away with his joy on their faces and peace in their hearts.

* * *

Given that the fullness of God was shown in Jesus, visualize the story again but this time replace the name *Jesus* with a name for God that helps you imagine the Father/Creator in his place. Names to insert might be *Love*, *Goodness*, *Creator*, the *Breath of Life*, or come up with your own. Let this new encounter enrich your understanding of the nature and character of the Creator God.

When you are finished, reflect on how imagining the Creator in Jesus's place influences your understanding of God.

* * *

Jesus said,
*"I have manifested your name
to the men whom you have given me
out of the world."*
John 17:6 (NKJV)

* * *

Story #10   Jesus Heals a Blind Man at Bethsaida

In Mark's Gospel, this story comes right after Jesus warned his disciples they should beware of the yeast of the Pharisees and Herod. "Yeast" is sometimes a metaphor for malice and wickedness. But the disciples didn't understand. They thought Jesus was telling them they had no bread to eat. Jesus expressed frustration with his disciples' inability to understand his comparisons. They were blind to what he meant, interpreting his words literally rather than figuratively. It's not accidental that Mark's next story shows Jesus opening the eyes of a blind man, an example of how Jesus helps his disciples to see or understand his meanings.

In this meditation, imagine you are the blind man. You have learned to lean heavily on your other physical senses to help compensate for not being able to see. Use your ears, nose, mouth, and hands to begin to understand what this story has to teach.

Take a moment to relax. Pray to be led by the Holy Spirit, and then enter into the story.

See – Listen – Taste – Smell – Touch

Mark 8:22–26

They came to Bethsaida. Some people brought a blind man to him and begged him to touch him. He took the blind man by the hand and led him out of the village.

Bethsaida is a town on the north edge of the Lake of Galilee. In the early mornings, you carefully count thirty-two steps down a path from the opening of your tiny hut. Once the path intersects with the road on the edge of the village, turn left and feel your way along the tables in the marketplace until you come to Caleb's booth. "I'm glad you're here today, Stephen," he says. He lets you help him clean the produce he will sell today. You're grateful for the work and for a fairly consistent source of food.

It's still early; the scraping feet of a donkey sends pebbles flying as it pulls a cart loaded with baskets of freshly baked bread. The tantalizing aroma fills the morning air. "Hi, Benjamin!" you shout. You know it's him because his donkey drags one foot as it walks. Another passing cart trails the scent of newly cut hay on its way to the livestock pens at the edge of town. Caged hens flutter and cackle their displeasure as another cart bounces over ruts in the dirt road. "Greetings, young story-teller!" the blacksmith bellows as he strolls by. Occasionally, someone drops a tasty fig into your lap.

As the morning progresses, a mixed scuffle feet approach you. The sandals of the first person to arrive slap the soles of his feet in his haste to execute a wildly spun plan. That's Jeremiah. He's always got a crazy idea to try. He says, "There's someone we want you to meet, Stephen. A Jewish rabbi who has a reputation for healing people is in the village. We want to see if he can help you to gain your sight." He and another friend grab you by the arms and lift you to your feet.

"Really, thanks, friends. But I don't need your help. I'm doing just fine." With great reluctance, you resist for about a forty yards. They ignore you and keep chattering like a pack of giddy teenagers. Something about their excitement turns your apprehension into tolerance, and then to hope.

After a twenty minute hike, Jeremiah whispers, "There he is!" Boldly approaching Jesus, they ask him to touch you. "Please help our friend to see. He's a good man."

Jesus says to you, "Give me your hand."

Hesitantly, you reach out your right hand into the open space in front of you. He grasps your wrist, gently but firmly. He takes a step toward you, turns and loops his arm above the elbow and between your arm and body. Holding you near him, he says nothing, but leads you away from the ones who brought you to him.

What is he doing? Why doesn't he do what he's going to do in the presence of my friends? But you're only a little concerned. You're accustomed to being led in many directions by many people.

And when he had put saliva on his eyes and laid his hands on him, he asked him, "Can you see anything?"

Jesus stops in a quiet place and releases your arm. He steps forward, rotates, and stands in front of you. He lifts his hands and squeezes the outer edges of your shoulders. "Stay where you are" is the message.

Then his hands slide upward from your shoulders and softly embrace your face. They are tender and warm, yet there are calluses on his palms. His breathing is slow and steady. Normally you would react to free yourself, but his touch is mesmerizing—so much so that when he places his moistened thumbs on your eyes, you don't flinch. He presses his thumbs on your eyelids. The pressure triggers fluctuating waves of light like ripples on a pond. Backing away, he asks, "Do you see anything?"

And the man looked up and said, "I can see people, but they look like trees, walking."
Then Jesus laid his hands on his eyes again; and he looked intently and his sight was restored, and he saw everything clearly.

Slowly, you raise your eyelids. Objects are blurry and without clear definition. Colors are subdued. A gasp comes from your gut as you try to comprehend how the images fit together. "Well, I'm not sure what I'm seeing. I see objects that are thick like a tree, and with branch-like projections. But they're moving, so they must be people."

Again Jesus places his hands on your face, presses his thumbs on your eyelids and then backs away. You open your eyes and this time things aren't as blurry. And the very first thing you see is Jesus—smiling at you. He's so ordinary looking. It would be easy to lose him in a crowd. Yet he is detached and separate from everything else. Then you turn your head and start examining things more closely. People aren't blending together anymore. Everyone isn't alike. You are starting to be able to tell them one from another.

New light floods into your consciousness. The images become fascinating. So many different shades and tints and blends and patterns. The variations are beautiful.

Then he sent him away to his home, saying, "Do not even go into the village."

Then Jesus says something strange to you. "Go home, but don't go back to the village."

Why? Your eyes have been opened! Shouldn't others be told? Especially the ones who brought you to him? *How can I keep this to myself, Jesus?*

Pause now and ask Jesus "why?" Why would he not want you to return to the village now that you can see all things clearly?

And ask why you couldn't see clearly the first time He touched you. What does he answer?

* * *

Given that the fullness of God was shown in Jesus, visualize the story again but this time replace the name *Jesus* with a name for God that helps you imagine the Father/Creator in his place. Names to insert might be *Love, Goodness, Creator*, the *Breath of Life*, or come up with your

own. Let this new encounter enrich your understanding of the nature and character of the Creator God.

When you are finished, reflect on how imagining the Creator in Jesus's place influences your understanding of God.

* * *

For it is the God who said,
"Let light shine out of darkness,"
who has shone in our hearts to give the light
of the knowledge of the glory of God
in the face of Jesus Christ.
2 Cor. 4:6

* * *

Story #11   Ten Healed of Leprosy

As learned in an earlier story, leprosy is a disease that deadens the nerve endings in the skin. You cannot feel pain when your hand is too near fire. If you are cutting vegetables with a knife, you may not realize you have cut a finger until you see blood on the cutting board.

Pain is a warning signal that something is not right in your body. Without pain, you cannot respond properly to real needs. To be fully human is to have feelings of pain as well as joy. True healing requires attending to the source from which the pain arises. In the following story, imagine yourself as one of the ten lepers who approach Jesus, asking for healing.

Take a moment to relax. Pray to be led by the Holy Spirit, and then enter into the story.

See – Listen – Taste – Smell – Touch

Luke 17:11–19

On the way to Jerusalem Jesus was going through the region between Samaria and Galilee. As he entered a village, ten lepers approached him. Keeping their distance, they called out, saying, "Jesus, Master, have mercy on us!"

Life was good for you until the day you noticed a deep tingling in your hands and feet. After some time the tingling went away. But another problem developed and today you walked through a narrow doorway, scraping your arm on a nail protruding from a board. Bright red blood dripped on the dirt floor from a nasty gash on your forearm. "Not another one! That's the third cut this week. This is getting worse." Flaps of torn skin turn red, then black, and then white. A rancid odor rises. When others are wounded, they cry out like little children. Yet you receive the same injuries without feeling any pain.

Why have I stopped feeling pain? The numbness covers over everything.

When you walk outside, you cover as much of your skin as you can, but others have noticed. Two women chat happily as they amble up the road but when they see you, they shy away, dropping their eyes and voices. They cover their faces and sneak a glance back at you when they pass. You're harmless, but they don't understand. Another man makes a wide path so as not to get near you.

Finally, someone reports you to the authorities. Neighbors stand outside your small house and shout for you to get out of the community. You might infect them. You don't want anyone to get this disease, but they aren't kind. . .and many were your friends. They say God is punishing you, that you did something to deserve this. *But I didn't do anything wrong.*

Outside the village, you live with others who are unable to feel anything, just like you. They push their way through life and act like nothing hurts them either. Jonathan over there has a new injury. His arm is disfigured, probably broken. He won't be able to plow his small plot of land next week. He sips from a wineskin he hides under his clothing. "I'm okay," he says. "Don't worry about me." Elizabeth wears that brightly colored wrap again. It has too much red thread in it for a decent woman to wear and her face paint doesn't cover up as much as she thinks it does. James always has those stupid jokes and laughs louder than is necessary. And Isaac never says anything. They're too busy covering up their wounds to notice yours. At least you don't feel judged by them.

If only I could feel the soft touch of a compassionate hand once again and feel alive. . .

Mary comes running up as a group of you sit around a fire. She's naïve and believes everything she hears. She says, "There's a new healer in the village. His name is Jesus. They say he can heal any disease or condition. Many people have asked him and he was willing to help. Come on, let's give it a try. He's at the crossroads on the way to Jerusalem. It's not too far." She insists, so you all stand and begin walking with her.

In the next village, Jesus stands talking to two men on the side of the road. From a distance, you call to him, "Jesus, I want to be able to feel again. Please, Jesus, help me." All the others call on him too. You're afraid he will ignore you. But no. He notices, and he answers...

When he saw them, he said to them, "Go and show yourselves to the priests." And as they went, they were made clean.

You reply, "Go to the priests? A lot of good that will do. They are the ones condemning us the most. This isn't going to work." Yet you turn and go with the group to show yourself to the religious leaders. You complain, "If he was going to heal us, why didn't he do it right there?"

Mary says, "We just have to trust and do what Jesus said."

James agrees with you, "They probably won't listen to us. They've got us labeled already. We didn't do anything wrong. I'm not sure I can take anymore criticism from those arrogant priests. I wish we didn't have to do this."

As you walk, a sensation shoots through your arm from a very old wound. *Ouch! What was that?* Then you notice that Jonathan begins to sob. His arm aches. Elizabeth takes off her flamboyant shawl and some ugly abrasions are exposed to the sun again. The unattended injuries of everyone begin to awaken, and they cry out to be soothed and treated instead of hidden. Pent up tears fall on crusty skin, and it becomes soft.

Then one of them, when he saw that he was healed, turned back, praising God with a loud voice. He prostrated himself at Jesus' feet and thanked him. And he was a Samaritan.

Everyone in your group asked for healing, and everyone has been healed. All have begun to feel again! Yes, there's pain, but even better, sweet joy! Wrap your arms around Jonathan. His body is warm, and his tears stop. Elizabeth and Mary clutch each other in elation and relief. "We're restored—clean in the eyes of all." "We have new life!" "There will still be ups and downs. . ." "We'll help each other." "We'll do all kinds of wonderful things together. We'll be nicer to those who have been excluded." "Except, wait a minute! Saddam isn't with us anymore. . ." "You're right. Where did he go?"

"Maybe it's better that he went his way. Since he's a foreigner with some unwelcome beliefs, the people in town might accept us more quickly if he's not with us."

Then Jesus asked, "Were not ten made clean? But the other nine, where are they? Was none of them found to return and give praise to God except this foreigner?" Then he said to him, "Get up and go on your way; your faith has made you well."

Breathing heavily, Saddam reaches the edge of the village where the group met Jesus. He slows and stops. Seeing a small group of people near a fig tree, he begins running again. Rushing between two men, he throws himself at Jesus's feet. "Thank you, Lord! Thank you! I hurt. You have made me able to feel again. I can't wait to feel the touch of my wife's hand, and my children. Thank you!"

"Didn't I make ten clean? Where are the others? Were none of them thankful to God except this man who is a foreigner?"

Extending his hand to help Saddam rise, Jesus says, "Get up and go on your way; your faith has made you well."

* * *

Given that the fullness of God was shown in Jesus, visualize the story again but this time replace the name *Jesus* with a name for God that helps you imagine the Father/Creator in his place. Names to insert might be *Love*, *Goodness*, *Creator*, the *Breath of Life*, or come up with your own. Let this new encounter enrich your understanding of the nature and character of the Creator God.

When you are finished, reflect on how imagining the Creator in Jesus's place influences your understanding of God.

* * *

*[Jesus] is the reflection of God's glory
and the exact imprint of God's very being.*
Hebrews 1:3 (NRSV)

* * *

Story #12   Jesus Raises a Widow's Son

With some exceptions, women were repressed as well as vulnerable. The laws of Moses included provisions to care for women if their husbands died. If a woman did not have children to care for her in old age, the deceased husband's brother was obligated to marry the widow so she would have food and shelter. If the deceased husband had no brother, and in the absence of any sons to care for her, the widow might have to turn to servant work or an unpleasant occupation to provide for her needs.

Imagine you are the widow in this story. Your husband has been dead for an undetermined length of time. And now your only son has died in the past twenty-four hours.

Take a moment to relax. Pray to be led by the Holy Spirit, and then enter into the story.

See – Listen – Taste – Smell – Touch

Luke 7:11–17

Soon [after healing a centurion's servant] *Jesus went to a town called Nain, and his disciples and a large crowd went with him. As he approached the gate of the town, a man who had died was being carried out. He was his mother's only son, and she was a widow; and with her was a large crowd from the town.*

This can't be happening. It's a dream. . .a very, very bad dream. People from the village slide softly into your one-room cottage. Many wail loudly, some for your son, some for you. "He was far too young to die" is repeated by all who ender. His best friend sobs pitifully, draping himself over the joyless form of your boy lying on the table. You rock back and forth on a short, three-legged stool. Shaking your head side to side, you try to cast out the thoughts about what is coming next. Moans rebound woefully in the bottom of the dried up well of your stomach, powerless to release an eerie and excruciating ache. To another visitor you say, "I know he is going to get up any minute now, to walk over and give me a hug."

A neighbor with three healthy sons approaches you. "I know someone else who lost a son. . ." Her voice evaporates into the dry air then returns, "So I know how you feel, but it will pass." *How can she think she knows how I feel? She's never lost a child. She has someone to help her.*

I want these selfish thoughts to go away. One moment, I think my stomach is going to twist so tight that I can't breathe. Then I start wondering: How am I going to support myself? A few supplies remain on a barren shelf. Some dried beans, a few figs. *How will I pay rent for this room that I call home? Where will I sleep when my landlord's mercy runs out? And how can I be thinking about myself at a time like this?*

"Thank you for coming, Sara," you say to a neighbor who puts her arm around you. "I wish our friend, Naomi, could be here, but it's too far from Capernaum and she can't get here in time."

Some neighbors are cooking stew and baking bread. The odors turn your stomach. *I never want to eat again.* The people in the village are nice people, but you've witnessed what happens. People will check on you for about three days, and then they'll forget you. Not because they are bad people. They simply can't change life back to the way it was for you. They feel helpless to make any difference. And they have to provide for their own needs. You've been in their shoes. But it's so different from this side, being the one left behind. *I have no one, nothing left to live for. My family was my life. There's no one left who needs me.*

Someone calls to you, "Ruth, it's time to go." That means it's time to make the dreaded walk to the town burial lot. "No!" comes a bizarre moan from your gut. "Don't make me do this." Your legs won't respond. Several men lift your boy off the table. You cry out, "Be careful, don't hurt my baby!" Like a dagger, reality pierces your heart again and again. "Why can't it be me? Let it be me." The women of the village surround you. They grip your arms to hold you up as they pull you to follow the men who carry your son out the door. The gate of the village appears closer than it usually does when you fetch water from the well. The burial grounds had always seemed so far away. *What's going to happen to me now?*

When the Lord saw her, he had compassion for her and said to her, "Do not weep."

When you step outside the village's entry gate, a man in a white robe holding a staff watches you. Others stand near him. Is he a rabbi? A Pharisee? You don't know if this is a good thing or not. You didn't make it to the synagogue as often as you should have. If you had enough strength to speak, you would ask only one question: "Why me? Why did God do this to me?" You hope this rabbi doesn't get involved. You're too numb to care what you've done right or wrong.

The teacher walks up to you. His eyes are soft, strangely soothing the emptiness in your soul. He's young, like your son. *I want to hold him. I need someone to hold...* so you wrap your arms around him and fall with all your weight on him. And he holds you. *I feel as light as a feather in his arms. Rest. I feel rest flowing from him.* A momentary oasis in your expanding wilderness. You're a little stronger now; maybe you can make it to the gravesite.

Then he came forward and touched the bier, and the bearers stood still. And he said, "Young man, I say to you, rise!" The dead man sat up and began to speak, and Jesus gave him to his mother.

Gently, the rabbi gives you to the women of the village. He walks over to the men carrying your son. What's he doing? He says something directly to your son; it sounds like, "Get up. . ." And your boy sits up!

Gasps and screams fill the air. What's happening? He's moving? He smiles like he's never smiled before! He's alive.

People run to touch him, to hug him, to tell others. They shout, "God of Abraham, a miracle, a miracle!" The rabbi laughs. Your mind is frantic: *I don't know what to do. Can this be real? I don't know what to believe anymore or who to hug first, the rabbi or my son. . . My son! My son! He was dead and now he is alive. I was dead, and now I am alive. Am I dreaming? Who is this man who told him to get up and live? How can I ever thank him?*

Fear seized all of them; and they glorified God, saying, "A great prophet has risen among us!" and "God has looked favorably on his people!" This word about him spread throughout Judea and all the surrounding country.

As quickly as mayhem erupted over the son sitting up, silence grips the crowd as all eyes turn and stare at Jesus. Several women clasp their hands and drop to their knees.

Your son kisses you on the cheek and says, "What's for dinner? I'm hungry." Sweet music to a mother's ears! "I'll fix you something right away." Grabbing Jesus's hand and holding between your hands, you say, "And Lord, please stay. Let me feed you too." He nods his head 'yes' and smiles.

"And son, when we've finished eating, please take me to Capernaum. I must tell my friend, Naomi, the good news! I must tell her what God has done for me."

* * *

Given that the fullness of God was shown in Jesus, visualize the story again but this time replace the name *Jesus* with a name for God that helps you imagine the Father/Creator in his place. Names to insert might be *Love*, *Goodness*, *Creator*, the *Breath of Life*, or come up with your own. Let this new encounter enrich your understanding of the nature and character of the Creator God.

When you are finished, reflect on how imagining the Creator in Jesus's place influences your understanding of God.

* * *

[Jesus] is the image of the invisible God,
the firstborn of all creation...
For in him all the fullness of God was pleased to dwell.
Colossians 1:15, 19

* * *

Story #13   Faith of a Canaanite Woman

The cities of Tyre and Sidon are coastal cities on the Mediterranean Sea in what is known today as Lebanon. Jesus, a Jew, interacts with a woman who was not a descendant of Abraham, Isaac, and Jacob. He's traveling on the fringes of the Promised Land, in territory taken by force from Canaanites.

Enter this story with the viewpoint of the woman as you approach a rabbi whose people pushed out your ancestors. They think you are inferior because you are not one of the chosen nation of Israel.

Take a moment to relax. Pray to be led by the Holy Spirit, and then enter into the story.

See – Listen – Taste – Smell – Touch

Matthew 15:21–28

Jesus left [Gennesaret] *and went away to the district of Tyre and Sidon. Just then a Canaanite woman from that region came out and started shouting, "Have mercy on me, Lord, Son of David; my daughter is tormented by a demon." But he did not answer her at all.*

Returning home from fetching water at the well, you unload to your sister, "My daughter is unmanageable. She's fine one day, then the next day, she's acts like she's out of her mind. She says and does things that don't make sense. I can't get her to wear appropriate clothes or speak respectfully to me or to say prayers to Asherah like my other children have learned to do. People talk about her. Something is not right with her. I've paid for every possible treatment available to get rid of the evil spirit within her."

"I remember," your sister consoles. "You've seen mediums, spiritual advisors, star gazers, and herbal merchants with no results. Nothing has been effective. You even took her to another country to try an unconventional therapy."

"Yes. I've sacrificed the family honor, name, tradition and my personal life. All this to find out I have no ability to make her conform. You know I just want what's best for her."

The mental and emotional anguish is deep. "What is causing this condition? What more can I do to help her? Did I bring this upon her? Is she like this because of something I did? Is Asherah unhappy with me?"

Your sister says, "I heard a rabbi is in town who casts out demons. He's an Israelite. Some say he's the son of David. I know what you think about Israelites, sister. They think they are so good. A righteous people."

Self-righteous, if you ask me...

"But the Galileans aren't as bad as their countrymen to the south in Judea. It doesn't matter; this miracle-working rabbi is in town and you're out of options with your daughter. You need to find him."

"Maybe you're right. I've heard about him, too. But I can't stand those people. I wouldn't do this if I had any other options. I'll go as soon as I drop off this water."

Having stored the water in your house, you walk the short distance into town. People you asked on the way said he's near the marketplace. *There he is, standing with four other men. How can I get his attention?*

"Lord, Son of David! Listen to me! I'm desperate. I need help!"

Jesus responds in a typical male, "chosen people" fashion: he looks away.

"Jesus! Listen to me! You're a Galilean who's a long way from Jerusalem. Whose rules are we to follow? Do you expect me to follow your uppity Israeli rules of order even when in a different land? Sorry, mister. We're on level ground here, and I know you're capable of healing my daughter. I'm not asking for anything for myself. She needs your help, otherwise I wouldn't bother with you. Why won't you listen to me? Aren't you supposed to be good? Or have I heard wrong?"

Those men with him must be his disciples. Maybe they will help. I've heard they, too, have been known to cast out demons. "Hey, you men. Will you help me. . .help my daughter?"

They stare at you. Unresponsive to your pleading. They turn away from you and talk in hushed tones among themselves. "I thought you were supposed to have some kind of healing powers. Show me—make me believe it's true."

And his disciples came and urged him, saying, "Send her away, for she keeps shouting after us." He answered, "I was sent only to the lost sheep of the house of Israel."

The heads of his disciples turn abruptly when Jesus says he has come to help bring only the people of Israel back to God. They ask him, "What do you mean, Jesus? If you were sent only to Israel, what are we doing outside Judea and Galilee, in Phoenicia? Are we looking for Jews who have left the faith, or for those who have moved away from the Promised Land?"

"Yet if you only came for the Israelites, why did you heal the Roman centurion's servant when he asked? We don't understand, Jesus."

But she came and knelt before him, saying, "Lord, help me." He answered, "It is not fair to take the children's food and throw it to the dogs." She said, "Yes, Lord, yet even the dogs eat the crumbs that fall from their masters' table."

You have heard too many stories that this rabbi is a good man. *My aggressive approach was wrong. I shouldn't treat a good man this way just because others of his tradition are hurtful. I must kneel and submit to his way of thinking and honor him for his position of authority.* Dropping to the hard ground in desperation, you beg, "Lord, help me."

He turns to face you and speaks, "Why should I use my power to help people who are not of my own faith? Why should I help anyone who doesn't believe what I think they should believe? Especially a heathen Canaanite?"

The hair on the back of your neck rises. Normally, you would get up, walk away, and never come back. *I'm treated better by people who have no religion or standards, but I have no other hope.* You respond, "Maybe so, Lord, but I have heard you are good, you are compassionate, you don't like to see anyone live in torment, and I know that is why you will help my daughter."

Then Jesus answered her, "Woman, great is your faith! Let it be done for you as you wish." And her daughter was healed instantly.

Jesus's jaw drops, the corners of his mouth raise, and his eyes sparkle. Not at your persistence, lots of people get things through persistence. Not at your belief in his power, lots of people have seen his power. He's delighted to hear your trust in his goodness, compassion, and mercy. He says, "Now I truly understand why you have come to me. You know me better than most of my own people know me. And you are right: I will help your daughter."

* * *

Given that the fullness of God was shown in Jesus, visualize the story again but this time replace the name *Jesus* with a name for God that helps you imagine the Father/Creator in his place. Names to insert might be *Love*, *Goodness*, *Creator*, the *Breath of Life*, or come up with your own. Let this new encounter enrich your understanding of the nature and character of the Creator God.

When you are finished, reflect on how imagining the Creator in Jesus's place influences your understanding of God.

*　*　*

Jesus said,
*"All things have been handed over to me by my Father;
and no one knows the Son except the Father,
and no one knows the Father except the Son
and anyone to whom the Son chooses to reveal him."*
Matthew 11:27

*　*　*

Story #14   Zacchaeus the Tax Collector

Tax collectors in Israel were despised. They were usually fellow countrymen who collected oppressive taxes for the Roman government. They were considered traitors to their own people and they often took advantage of their position, raising the amount of tax they collected for personal gain.

Zacchaeus, a tax collector, was a short man. People looked down on him in many ways. Try to imagine yourself in his place and let the Spirit show you how the story of Zacchaeus can illuminate your understanding of God and yourself.

Take a moment to relax. Pray to be led by the Holy Spirit, and then enter into the story.

See – Listen – Taste – Smell – Touch

Luke 19:1–10

[Jesus] entered Jericho and was passing through it. A man was there named Zacchaeus; he was a chief tax collector and was rich. He was trying to see who Jesus was, but on account of the crowd he could not, because he was short in stature. So he ran ahead and climbed a sycamore tree to see him, because he was going to pass that way.

Sitting on your balcony, Jericho waits for the dawn of another hot day. A slave brings you a cup of water. A rare breeze freshens the air as the morning sun burns in the eastern sky. You've been up a couple of hours already because sleep is as elusive as a frightened lamb. Your thoughts go to the party you hosted last night: an ambassador from Rome, an emissary from Jerusalem, a traveling delegation from Egypt, and a few token locals. Born into a poor Jewish family, now you have wealth, power, prestige. *What more could I want?* A little respect might be nice.

The governing authorities respect your ability to generate revenues for them. But you know they have no loyalty to anyone. Your money ought to generate some respect from the local people. You regularly host social functions and sponsor community activities. But just because people attend your functions doesn't mean they respect you. Collecting taxes for Rome may not make you popular but someone's got to do it. They don't understand what it takes to succeed, nor does it matter. That's why it's not hard to take their money.

In one conversation last night, you heard some stories about Jesus of Nazareth. He's a preacher, a healer. He's helped a lot of people. You heard he's not the typical street corner preacher who announces the condemnation of God. You avoid personal contact with religious Jews. Religious people always get in your way. You used to go to the synagogue as a child. But if God is nothing more than a bunch of rules and demands, how different is that from the Roman empire?

Yet, there is something unusual about this Jesus. People are attracted to him, not because he demands attention, but because he's helping them in their sickness and poverty. They're falling all over him, willing to do anything for him. He must have some kind of gimmick, a deal they can't refuse. It's obviously working, but oddly, it doesn't sound like he's taking advantage of it, and people have nothing bad to say about him. They actually like him, even though he's pushing religion. They can't stop talking about him. He sounds too good to be true. What does he want from people? No one does anything without wanting something in return.

Last night they said he's staying with friends and plans to say a few words today outside Elisha's spring, which isn't far away. You've heard enough about him; now it's time to see for yourself.

Finishing the last bite of a juicy pomegranate, you stand and hurry out the door.

I wish I'd started earlier, there's already a crowd around him, and he's not quite to the spring... It's always been hard for you to listen to people when you can't see their eyes, facial expressions, body language—and you're used to front row seats anyway. You start running on the outside edge of the crowd.

There's a tree close to the place where orators speak, another fifty yards ahead. Catching your breath, you think, *I'll just climb up to that first branch.* That's not as easy as it sounds. You're wearing the Persian outer cloak you purchased on your last trip to Sidon. It fits nicely and you don't want to damage it. Throwing the robe over one of the branches, you jump and grab onto the lowest branch.

Ouch. You're not as nimble as you used to be and not accustomed to this kind of exertion. The soft tissue of your palms tears as you strain to pull a well-fed torso onto the first limb. Stinging abrasions on your arms and legs cry out. *Why am I doing this?* A sharp pain shoots from your lower back as you shimmy one branch higher in the tree. *Is all this worth it?* Good, you made it and with scarcely enough time to catch your breath. Soon, you see Jesus coming down the narrow street surrounded by wide-eyed peasants clinging to him like prickly seeds.

When Jesus came to the place, he looked up and said to him, "Zacchaeus, hurry and come down; for I must stay at your house today." So he hurried down and was happy to welcome him. All who saw it began to grumble and said, "He has gone to be the guest of one who is a sinner."

Jesus walks directly to the base of the tree, stops and looks up. Blood rises to your face and you feel like a child.

Smiling, he says, "What's a grown man doing in a tree in his best clothes, nursing his cuts and abrasions?"

Sheepishly, you smile back at him.

Then he calls you by your name. "Zacchaeus."

How does he know my name? Is this a good thing or a bad thing?

"How about if I stay at your house tonight?"

"What? You want to stay at my house? You want to eat a meal with me?" *That means he wants to get to know me. . .and wants me to know him. And he does this openly for all to see.* "I'd be honored, Lord." *If he knows me, he knows I'm a tax collector, despised by most. I don't know what to think.* Forgetting your cloak, you slide off the lower branch and hit the dirt with a thud.

Jesus puts his arm around you and asks about your family. The crowd follows, most of them grumbling now, whispering their disgust that Jesus would sink so low as to spend time with a sinner who isn't going to change his ways. Why would a person of God associate with a man who turned his back on his own people, and doesn't practice the rules of his own religion? Doesn't Jesus know how bad that looks?

Zacchaeus stood there and said to the Lord, "Look, half of my possessions, Lord, I will give to the poor; and if I have defrauded anyone of anything, I will pay back four times as much." Then Jesus said to him, "Today salvation has come to this house, because he too is a son of Abraham. For the Son of Man came to seek out and to save the lost."

Imagine this! A man of God eating with you in your own house. He certainly isn't like the other religious hypochondriacs who think they'll catch something evil from you. Jesus laughs and tells about the time he fell from a tree when he was growing up and lets you know you ought to send someone to get your cloak hanging in the sycamore tree. "I meant to leave it there," you say, and he laughs again. This man is truly different, special. You would gladly listen to him. You tell him that you've heard some stories, that he's been helping people in the area. You ask him about the work he's been doing locally. So he tells you.

"You've been helping the poor? I'll do the same. You've honored me, Lord, and I want to return your favor. You're a man who's doing good for the sake of good. I want to do the same. Things are going to be different around my house. There are many ways I can be of help to others too. I've only just begun to think of them all."

"Zacchaeus, I promise you won't regret it. When you do this, you will find meaning and purpose in your life that you have never had. May God bless and guide your efforts."

* * *

Given that the fullness of God was shown in Jesus, visualize the story again but this time replace the name *Jesus* with a name for God that helps you imagine the Father/Creator in his place. Names to insert might be *Love*, *Goodness*, *Creator*, the *Breath of Life*, or come up with your own. Let this new encounter enrich your understanding of the nature and character of the Creator God.

When you are finished, reflect on how imagining the Creator in Jesus's place influences your understanding of God.

* * *

*The LORD is good to all,
and his compassion
is over all that he has made.*
Psalm 145:9

* * *

Story #15 Woman Caught in Adultery

By the time Jesus lived in Israel, there were many religious opinions about how to enforce the penalties prescribed in the law for adultery. Most people who were caught were not automatically put to death.[6] This story is not about labeling one specific sin as worse than another. Every sin carries the sentence of death, a spiritual death that separates us from the abundant life God wants for us.

Imagine yourself as the woman caught in adultery. Focus your attention on Jesus. Try to understand his reactions and the way he deals with sin.

Take a moment to relax. Pray to be led by the Holy Spirit, and then enter into the story.

See – Listen – Taste – Smell – Touch

John 8:2–11
Early in the morning [Jesus] came again to the temple. All the people came to him and he sat down and began to teach them. The scribes and the Pharisees brought a woman who had been caught in adultery; and making her stand before all of them, they said to him, "Teacher, this woman was caught in the very act of committing adultery. Now in the law Moses commanded us to stone such women. Now what do you say?" They said this to test him, so that they might have some charge to bring against him.

The viselike grip of your accusers pinches your upper arms. Blood vessels burst under your skin as they jerk you into the temple courtyard. An old woman in the gathering crowd spits on you and the slimy liquid slides down your neck. You wipe it with the border of your mantle. Your shame clings to you like tar to cloth. Children laugh and point fingers at you. You've been in their place, pointing your finger at alcoholics, thieves, and Sabbath-breakers. The irony is clear and still you resist being identified with those who break the law. *It's not fair! They set me up. My business is none of your business!*

A Pharisee shouts, "You are guilty of bringing shame upon yourself and your family!" Everyone in the village will soon know. You had so much going for you. Your parents were proud of you. They will be devastated. Your children will never understand. Your husband... *If he had paid more attention to me, this wouldn't have happened. It's his fault that I succumbed to the affections of a suitor. It was only going to be a short term thing. I planned to keep things under control.* No one cares about your weak excuses.

Where's your partner in this sin? Why didn't they drag him with you? It's his sin too. *Why do I suffer this guilt alone? Not fair, not fair.* Your hair falls like a dark and stringy shield over your streaked face. Your eyes seek a hiding place.

Yet in your disgrace, you see through the guise of the religious leaders. *It's my bad luck that the leaders of this sect of Judaism found me out. They love to throw stones.* They are using you to advance their own agenda against the new rabbi. "This is how we'll get him!" they said. They don't care about you. A young Pharisee follows your every move. He would as readily succumb to your physical affections as he would stone you. In a smug display, they fling you to the ground in front of Jesus. The sharp edges of small rocks cut your palms and forearms as you break your fall. Dust flies up in your face and the taste of it on your lips makes you gag. Sheep have been through here recently.

Jesus bent down and wrote with his finger on the ground. When they kept on questioning him, he straightened up and said to them, "Let anyone among you who is without sin be the first to throw a stone at her." And once again he bent down and wrote on the ground.

Your accusers grip their rocks, waiting for the rabbi's signal. You cower, knowing they need to make an example of someone. Any second, the rocks will start pelting your back and head. But Jesus is slow to respond. What is he doing? Lifting your head and moving your hair away to see, he's writing on the ground with his finger. *Did he not hear them? Does he not understand what I did?* The law clearly states a punishment—stoning. *Get it over with. Maybe they'll be doing me a favor. How can I live with this shame?* As you lower your head, Jesus stands. His shadow shields you from the burning rays of the noon sun. You await his condemnation and scorn, fearing he will sanction their penalty. He speaks. *What? What did he say?*

Whoever hasn't sinned can throw the first stone? You know some of these men and you know they aren't perfect. Yet it takes only one to start a barrage of stones flying. Blood trickles from a scrape on the back of your hand. Jesus squats down and writes on the ground again.

When they heard it, they went away, one by one, beginning with the elders; and Jesus was left alone with the woman standing before him.

A heavy rock strikes the ground. You wrap your arms tighter around your head. Another rock hits the ground...and another rock hits the ground further away. You still can't look up. The thought of a rock striking your face keeps your nose in the dirt. But now, even the harsh crowd slips away. What's going on? It's strangely quiet...

Jesus straightened up and said to her, "Woman, where are they? Has no one condemned you?" She said, "No one, sir." And Jesus said, "Neither do I condemn you. Go your way, and from now on, do not sin again."

Jesus rises and moves to stand in front of you. Slowly raising your head, you look to one side and then the other, and then behind you. Your accusers are gone. Every one of them is gone.

Realizing the attack is no longer imminent, your shoulders tremble, your stomach convulses, and you vomit as the people Jesus had been teaching watch. Jesus speaks, "Woman, where are they? Has no one thrown a stone and condemned you?"

Looking into Jesus's eyes, you say, "No one, sir. Who are you? Why didn't they stone me now, in front of you?"

Jesus says, "I don't condemn you."

"What? You're a man of God! And you don't condemn me? You know I'm guilty. My husband will never forgive me. I've shamed my family. How will I live with myself? So what do I do now? What do I do now?"

"Your poor choices carry a penalty of their own. Unfortunately, you will have to suffer those consequences. Yet I come and teach in this place often. If you need help, come to me. As for the sin that brought this trouble to you, don't do it anymore."

* * *

Given that the fullness of God was shown in Jesus, visualize the story again but this time replace the name *Jesus* with a name for God that helps you imagine the Father/Creator in his place. Names to insert might be *Love*, *Goodness*, *Creator*, the *Breath of Life*, or come up with your own. Let this new encounter enrich your understanding of the nature and character of the Creator God.

When you are finished, reflect on how imagining the Creator in Jesus's place influences your understanding of God.

* * *

*In their case the god of this world
has blinded the minds of the unbelievers,
to keep them from seeing the light
of the gospel of the glory of Christ,
who is the image of God.*
2 Cor. 4:4

* * *

Story #16   Jesus Heals a Boy with an Unclean Spirit

How much belief does it take to be healed, to bring healing to others, or to be saved? Are there different levels of belief? Keep these questions in mind as you participate in this story, remembering that the Greek word for "believe" is also translated as "trust." Many people in this story exhibit trust and lack of trust. Can you trust and not trust at the same time?

Imagine yourself as the man whose son has been possessed by an unclean spirit since birth. Think about how it might relate to someone close to you who you would like to be made whole. What does it mean to have belief that brings healing?

Take a moment to relax. Pray to be led by the Holy Spirit, and then enter into the story.

See – Listen – Taste – Smell – Touch

Mark 9:14–29
When [Jesus, Peter, James, and John] *came to the disciples, they saw a great crowd around them, and some scribes arguing with them. When the whole crowd saw him, they were immediately overcome with awe, and they ran forward to greet him.* [Jesus] *asked them, "What are you arguing about with them?" Someone from the crowd answered him, "Teacher, I brought you my son; he has a spirit that makes him unable to speak; and whenever it seizes him, it dashes him down; and he foams and grinds his teeth and becomes rigid; and I asked your disciples to cast it out, but they could not do so."*

Three of your neighbors told you they have seen or heard that Jesus of Nazareth gives sight to the blind, heals the sick, raises the dead, and casts out evil spirits. You know it's true. You've had friends experience his healing touch. *If only it could happen for me...* For years, you've searched for answers to help your son. You've brought him to the priests. They say there's no hope for him. It's like he goes into a trance, and when you speak to him, he refuses to tell you what's wrong. His eyes roll to the top of his head; then he shudders and begins to shake. When it happens, the muscles in your throat tighten and you can't swallow. What's wrong with him? Maybe Jesus can help him. Today you decide to find this Jesus; you won't settle for anything less. No one's going to talk you out of it.

You take the time to put a nice robe on Nathan so he's presentable. He's usually calm in the mornings. He smiles weakly as you brush his hair. He walks at a slower pace than you, and you encourage him often along the way. After forty-five minutes, you've looked in all the places people said Jesus could be found. You ask others if they know about Jesus and where he might be. They tell you a few of his disciples are in the marketplace. So you hurry to town, pulling Nathan along.

Judas and Thomas are bartering with a vendor as you approach them. "Please, sirs, have mercy and help release this evil spirit from my son." Compassionately, they back away from their business, get on their knees, close their eyes, and lay their hands on him. Nothing happens. They proclaim some beautiful words that surely will cast out a demon, and nothing happens. Heads turn in the market; several people wander over and gather around you. Some of the local scribes start giving the father advice. "You must go to the temple. Buy a lamb and sacrifice it to God. Do the correct religious things. Then obey the commandments. God is punishing him for the wrong his parents have done. These sicknesses don't happen to people who keep the commandments."

A squeal of delight erupts from the back of the crowd, and all eyes turn toward Jesus as he approaches with three disciples. You've never met Jesus personally, so you wouldn't have recognized him on your own. You haven't had time to get involved in religious details because of Nathan. Jesus isn't as tall as you imagined. You thought he would be taller and a little more noticeable. He looks like an average person, at best. Yet everyone says he's the one who can help.

He answered them, "You faithless generation, how much longer must I be among you? How much longer must I put up with you? Bring him to me."

The irritation in Jesus's voice rubs like sandpaper on sensitive skin. *Who's he talking to? Me? The religious law keepers? His own disciples? Faithless? Without trust?* "Just tell me, what do I have to trust in to get my son healed? Tell me, and then you won't have to put up with me anymore. I have no other hope."

And they brought the boy to him. When the spirit saw him, immediately it convulsed the boy, and he fell on the ground and rolled about, foaming at the mouth. Jesus asked the father, "How long has this been happening to him?" And he said, "From childhood. It has often cast him into the fire and into the water, to destroy him; but if you are able to do anything, have pity on us and help us."

Nathan gazes downward as Judas and Thomas gently lead him to Jesus. As he lifts his eyes, his knees buckle and he slips out of the disciples' grasp. Seeing the boy jerk and shudder on the ground, his father rushes to his aid, cradling him to keep his face out of the dirt. "Ever since he was a child, Jesus, I have taught him the commandments of Moses, but he doesn't understand them. I've done everything I've been told to do. Nothing helps. The more I push, the more he resists, and the consequences keep getting worse. Is God punishing me? My son's done nothing. He doesn't deserve to suffer like this. Jesus, if you are able to do anything, have pity on us and help us."

Jesus said to him, "If you are able! —All things can be done for the one who believes." Immediately the father of the child cried out, "I believe; help my unbelief!"

Tears run down your cheeks as you wait for a response. You know Jesus must be good; he's helped others in your situation. But can he help your son? His disciples have already tried and failed.

You notice that your son's eyes have glazed over again, and his shoulders begin to squeeze close to his body. You pull him gently to your chest. *I've smelled too many burned clothes, tended too much seared and wounded skin, and washed out too many bloody stains through the years.*

Maybe it's not the disciples. Maybe it's you. Maybe your son is suffering for your lack of faith. It's hard to have faith after so many failures.

"'If *you* are able'!" Jesus punctuates that *you* with a raised eyebrow. "All things can be done for the one who believes."

"I believe!" you burst out. "But help my unbelief," you beg.

When Jesus saw that a crowd came running together, he rebuked the unclean spirit, saying to it, "You spirit that keeps this boy from speaking and hearing, I command you, come out of him, and never enter him again!" After crying out and convulsing him terribly, it came out, and the boy was like a corpse, so that most of them said, "He is dead."

Vendors and shoppers from the market dash toward the commotion. People push and shove each other trying to get a better perspective. What's the rabbi going to do now? Focusing his eyes on Nathan, Jesus commands the tormenting spirit within him to leave, telling it never to return. Like others have said, these spirits cling tightly. After what feels like an eternity, Nathan finally stops shaking.

He stops resisting. There is nothing more to fight against. Free of that unclean spirit, peace is all that remains.

Some in the crowd shout, "The boy is dead—he's not moving"...as if when a person isn't doing something, he must be dead. Do ugly and frightening actions prove you're alive?

> *But Jesus took him by the hand and lifted him up, and he was able to stand. When he had entered the house, his disciples asked him privately, "Why could we not cast it out?" He said to them, "This kind can come out only through prayer."*

A miracle! Jesus lifts Nathan gently to his feet. Your son is now able to stand on his own. *I believe God is good. I believe Jesus is good. I want to believe in such a way that I can keep my boy safe and whole.*

The disciples enter a house with Jesus. You follow and overhear them asking, "Jesus, why couldn't we drive out the unclean spirit?"

Jesus quietly says, "This kind needs prayer."

"Jesus, we did pray! We said the words you taught us. Whose prayers? Ours? Yours? The parent's prayers? The community's prayers? In the state he was in, the boy certainly couldn't help himself, could he? Whose prayers?"

* * *

With the fullness of God shown in Jesus, visualize the story again but this time replace the name *Jesus* with a name for God that helps you imagine the Father/Creator in his place: *Love, Goodness, Creator*, the *Breath of Life*, or come up with your own. Let this new encounter enrich your understanding of the nature and character of the Creator God.

Reflect on how imagining the Creator in Jesus's place influences your understanding of God.

* * *

Jesus said,
*"It is written in the prophets,
'And they shall all be taught by God.'"*
John 6:45

* * *

Story #17   Jesus Heals the Official's Son

Jesus returns to the area in which he grew up, Galilee. It was like coming home for Jesus. Yet, hometown folks are often fickle. When it's to their advantage to claim him as their own, he's a hero. But the sense of familiarity can also breed contempt.

Imagine yourself as the royal official who asks for healing for his son. Try to develop a feeling toward Jesus that comes from living in the same region in which he grew up—almost like you went to the same high school or college, or were born into a common tradition. Interact with Jesus. Ask him questions during your meditation. Does coming from the same hometown as Jesus affect his response to you?

Take a moment to relax. Pray to be led by the Holy Spirit, and then enter into the story.

See – Listen – Taste – Smell – Touch

John 4:43–53

When the two days were over, [Jesus] *went from that place* [Judea] *to Galilee (for Jesus himself had testified that a prophet has no honor in the prophet's own country). When he came to Galilee, the Galileans welcomed him, since they had seen all that he had done in Jerusalem at the festival; for they too had gone to the festival.*

Stories abounded of Jesus in the small towns and villages of Galilee, many of them made up of a few shelters constructed near each other. Reports circulated, even from Jerusalem, about his healings and his teachings. A young man from Galilee is making a mark in the big city. Residents of your native land swell with pride and say, "Maybe those city-folks will show us a little more respect. We aren't as off-the-beaten-path as some might think."

Recently, in a small village where you visited with the men in leadership, one said, "Did you hear Jesus of Nazareth came through three days ago? I told him, 'Great job in Jerusalem, Jesus! You made us proud when we heard that you healed those lepers. How did you do it?'"

Another interrupted, saying, "And I said, 'Jesus, stay and eat some bread and some wine with us and tell us more about your adventures. We want to hear more about what you've done.' And he stayed with us for the afternoon."

Then he came again to Cana in Galilee where he had changed the water into wine. Now there was a royal official whose son lay ill in Capernaum. When he heard that Jesus had come from Judea to Galilee, he went and begged him to come down and heal his son, for he was at the point of death. Then Jesus said to him, "Unless you see signs and wonders you will not believe."

Very little has changed in Cana. The well dug a hundred years ago still has a broken edge where mortar has deteriorated and rocks have fallen from their original settings. As you enter after walking for five hours over rolling terrain, several vendors are positioned on the side of the road. A villager waves and then continues talking to his neighbor, "Jesus returned yesterday. He certainly showed us a good time at Judah and Rebecca's wedding, didn't he? I'm glad I was there because I'd never have believed it without tasting it for myself."

As a government official living in Capernaum, appointed to the Galilean position by Herod because of your knowledge of the region, your job is to administer the newest edicts handed down by Rome. Government rules help to keep order and unruly people under control.

A week ago, your son, Jacob, became nauseated and worsened into diarrhea. He stopped playing with the other children. His skin is ashen. No herbs are helping. He's eaten nothing for two days. When you left Capernaum, he was lying in bed and didn't stir or open his eyes. You were afraid to leave home this morning, but you are required to deliver a report on Cana to your superiors on the sixth day of the week. You can make the trip with one overnight if Cana is the only site you assess.

A grisly old man passes by, leading a burro with baskets tied to its back. "Sir," you ask, "The sun is directly overhead. Have you heard where Jesus might be this time of day? I was hoping to find him before meet with your town leaders."

He mutters, "You might look around the wood shop. He visits there often, but don't expect much. The rumors about him are a little exaggerated."

You hurry to the tree-lined east side of town and make your way up a narrow path leading to the wood shop. As you reach the crest of the hill, Jesus is helping the carpenter, who is one of your friends from childhood. Sweating profusely, Jesus handles one end of the large saw. You know they're cutting cedar because it smells like the beams in your home. "Greetings, Jonathan. I've come to see Jesus."

"Jesus, I live in Capernaum now and my boy is very sick." Jesus stops, reaches for a piece of cloth to wipe his face, and says, "I suppose you, too, need a sign, a miracle, and then you will trust."

"What do you mean, Jesus? I came here because I'm desperate and I think you can help me. I've heard stories that you've helped others. I'm not here to test you, Jesus. My son is deathly ill and I need help."

Jesus nods once and you continue.

"People from many regions have said you have the power to help. Why would I doubt them? I'm not like the locals around here. Yes, I've heard some cynical remarks, but maybe they haven't heard what I've heard. I might have come earlier, but I thought the herbs would help. I don't know what else to do."

The official said to him, "Sir, come down before my little boy dies." Jesus said to him, "Go; your son will live." The man believed the word that Jesus spoke to him and started on his way.

"I beg you, Jesus. I'm afraid he will die. Please help me."

Jesus puts his hand on your shoulder and says, "Go, your son will live."

"I'd be glad to pay you, Lord. I don't expect you to help for free. When can you come?" Jesus grabs the saw handle again and says, "It's okay. I don't have to come with you. Your boy is going to be fine. Trust me."

"Trust you? Don't you have to come and touch him or pray for him?"

"No. That's not necessary. Your boy will be fine."

Wrapping your arms around Jesus and with relief in your voice, you say, "You're the healer. I have no reason to question your word. I'm so grateful, Jesus. I won't forget this."

Hurrying into Cana, you send word for the town leaders to gather so you can get your business finished. Waiting for everyone to arrive takes longer than collecting the necessary information. At least you won't be traveling in the heat of the day.

As you complete your work, you see the sun falling quickly. That means you'll be able to walk only a few miles before it gets dangerous. Thieves come out at night, and it's fourteen miles over hilly terrain to get home. You'll stop at a small village you've stayed in before.

As he was going down, his slaves met him and told him that his child was alive. So he asked them the hour when he began to recover, and they said to him, "Yesterday at one in the afternoon the fever left him." The father realized that this was the hour when Jesus had said to him, "Your son will live." So he himself believed, along with his whole household.

A crowing rooster announces a day that still has not shown itself. With a jolt you sit up. *Where am I? Oh yes, I left Cana last night. I haven't slept this deeply in a week. I can't wait to see my son.* Grabbing your bag, you leave a token for the kind folks who took you in. The goat they roasted last night was delicious. *These are good people around here.* Throwing a light cloak around your shoulders to break the chill, you hurry to the east where a trace of light signals a new day.

Three miles from home, several people who work for you run to meet you. Skidding to a stop, they gasp, "Your son! Your son! Something wonderful has happened. We couldn't wait for your arrival. He's going to be okay! He's better."

"Are you certain? How do you know? I was hoping, but tell me precisely what happened and when it happened. This is important. I need to know the details."

"It was when the sun was high in the sky, and Jacob opened his eyes for the first time in two days. One of the neighbors brought some drippings from her Acacia tree. We put it on some bread and encouraged him to eat a little. He drank some water, and a short time later, he sat up on the edge of the bed. Then he asked if he could go outside to see his friends. Once your wife stopped hugging him, she let him go outside for a few minutes. "

"Praise God! It's true! I don't know how I knew it would be. I felt it inside, and I've got a story of my own to tell you as we continue home. I want to see Jacob and hug him for myself." Picking up your pace, you begin, "You knew I was in Cana yesterday. Well, I was entering town and asked a man coming out, 'I heard that the healer, Jesus, is in town, where can I find him?'"

"You didn't!"

"Yes, I did!"

"And what happened next?"

* * *

Given that the fullness of God was shown in Jesus, visualize the story again but this time replace the name *Jesus* with a name for God that helps you imagine the Father/Creator in his place. Names to insert might be *Love*, *Goodness*, *Creator*, the *Breath of Life*, or come up with your own. Let this new encounter enrich your understanding of the nature and character of the Creator God.

When you are finished, reflect on how imagining the Creator in Jesus's place influences your understanding of God.

O TASTE AND SEE

* * *

*Do you despise the riches of His goodness,
forbearance, and longsuffering,
not knowing that the goodness of God
leads you to repentance?
Romans 2:4 (NKJV)*

* * *

Story #18   Samaritan Opposition

People rejected Jesus from the beginning. King Herod tried to destroy him when he was born. The scribes and Pharisees continued the resistance when Jesus did not abide by religious laws as they interpreted them. Even those outside the chosen people of Israel participated in the rejection. Yet Jesus set his face toward his ultimate mission: to reveal the goodness of God and God's love for all creation. Walk alongside Jesus in this story. Do you see yourself in any of these responses to Jesus?

Take a moment to relax. Pray to be led by the Holy Spirit, and then enter into the story.

See – Listen – Taste – Smell – Touch

Luke 9:51–62

When the days drew near for [Jesus] to be taken up, he set his face to go to Jerusalem. And he sent messengers ahead of him. On their way they entered a village of the Samaritans to make ready for him; but they did not receive him, because his face was set toward Jerusalem.

You've been following Jesus for almost three years. Often you've seen him cheerful, sometimes teasing. One time, you called him Rabbi "Spontaneous." If the wind blew towards the west, he'd say, "Something tells me we need to go to Sidon... Let's go, friends." He'd get a twinkle in his eyes like a new adventure was beginning. But the past few days, his demeanor is different. He stares into the distance, his manner solemn. A destiny draws him, the way nature draws a boulder down a mountainside. Nothing can divert the rock as it rolls toward Jerusalem. "This is why I came," he says. Everything else has been secondary.

Jesus motions to James, John, and you, "Go ahead to the next Samaritan village. Let them know we are on our way to Jerusalem. We're going to the temple, but tell them I have some good news to share with them."

You pack a bag and sling it over your shoulder, pick up your walking stick, and hurry to catch up with James and John. "How do you think this village will receive us?"

John slaps a fly away from his ear and says, "I'm not sure. Some villages still have a centuries old chip on their shoulder." All of you know the prejudice that developed against Samaritans when the Israelites taken captive to Babylon returned from exile. Jews living away from Jerusalem who escaped being taken ended up marrying women of other nations. They built their own place and style of worship instead of worshipping at the temple in Jerusalem. They were accused of departing from the true faith.

John continues, "Most Samaritans say they don't need any arrogant Israelite rabbi to tell them how to live their lives. Let's just say this: Don't expect too much."

You follow the narrow path for a half hour before passing through a stand of camelthorn shrubs that borders the village. The village leader squats with arms folded next to two older men. It looks like they've been building a small house. You approach and say, "We follow of Jesus of Nazareth. He's a rabbi on his way to Jerusalem but he would like to stop here and share some good news with you."

He looks at all three of you, turns his head and spits on the ground. Then he turns to you and shakes his head 'no.' Having been treated the way you expected, you return to where you left Jesus.

"Jesus, they don't want to listen to you."

When his disciples James and John saw it, they said, "Lord, do you want us to command fire to come down from heaven and consume them?" But he turned and rebuked them. Then they went on to another village.

True to their reputation, the brothers nicknamed "the sons of thunder" react. With arms flailing, they cry, "Jesus, you are the Messiah! These infidels ought to pay for their disrespect of you. You've done nothing to deserve their disdainful rejection. Don't they know who you are? Let us show them the wrath of God just like Elijah did to that king in Samaria who turned to false gods. We'd be delighted to call down fire from heaven to destroy anyone who rejects you, Jesus. Then all people will fear your power and judgment, and we'll be like those prophets of old who showed the world who's the boss! We want to help you crush them."

Jesus takes a deep breath, lays down the knife he was using to whittle a figurine out of a piece of wood, and responds, "Think about what you are saying. Have you *ever* seen me use my power like that? Have you seen me use my power for anything other than for good? Are you not paying attention? Have you not learned anything about me yet?"

The darts of Samaritan rejection bounce off Jesus like unripe grapes thrown against a fencepost. "I have come to bring good news to all people. When the Creator reigns in your life, you will know that you won't have to defend him or me."

As they were going along the road, someone said to him, "I will follow you wherever you go." And Jesus said to him, "Foxes have holes, and birds of the air have nests; but the Son of Man has nowhere to lay his head."

The pace increases as you and your associates hike toward Jerusalem. Ahead wait the busy streets filled with activity and people. Speaking to people you meet along the road excites you. People notice the rabbi you follow and tell you how they have heard of Jesus's goodness. Stories about him spread like wild fire in a dry land.

They've heard he is kind and caring and able to help them. They come up to him like cautious sheep approaching a watering hole, and once they encounter him, they no longer fear taking a drink. He quenches their thirst.

A man previously healed by him falls on his knees and pledges his allegiance to Jesus. "You don't know what that means, young man. To follow me means detaching yourself from everything. If you follow me, you can't get settled, as if you have arrived and that's all there is. Any place we pause is only a brief respite before the true goal."

To another he said, "Follow me." But he said, "Lord, first let me go and bury my father." But Jesus said to him, "Let the dead bury their own dead; but as for you, go and proclaim the kingdom of God." Another said, "I will follow you, Lord; but let me first say farewell to those at my home." Jesus said to him, "No one who puts a hand to the plow and looks back is fit for the kingdom of God."

A man comes near and claims he will follow Jesus, but then says, "My father is elderly and that takes a lot of my time." A woman says, "My kids are young and that takes so much of my time." A synagogue worker says, "My brothers and sisters will think I'm shunning them if I tell them I am busy doing religious work and can't attend the usual family functions. They won't approve of me, Jesus, if I put you ahead of family. Neither will my friends, coworkers, neighbors. No one will understand if I don't put them first. They'll think I've gone off the deep end and become a religious fanatic." To yourself, you admit you've used some of these same excuses. They sound weak coming from others.

Jesus brushes a lock of hair away from his face, looks into their eyes, and says, "I know your excuses. You will always have excuses for why you cannot follow me at this time."

He knows them better than they know themselves. You're tired of their excuses too— after all, you gave up your career. Maybe a little fire from heaven is what they need to wake up. Whatever he does to them, they'll deserve it. Instead, Jesus says, "Make a decision. Your excuses won't bring you true life. You deceive yourself, not me. What I have to offer is of far greater value than the artificial treasures in your possession now."

* * *

Given that the fullness of God was shown in Jesus, visualize the story again but this time replace the name *Jesus* with a name for God that helps you imagine the Father/Creator in his place. Names to insert might be *Love*, *Goodness*, *Creator*, the *Breath of Life*, or come up with your own. Let this new encounter enrich your understanding of the nature and character of the Creator God.

When you are finished, reflect on how imagining the Creator in Jesus's place influences your understanding of God.

O TASTE AND SEE

* * *

Oh, give thanks to the LORD,
for He is good!
For His mercy endures forever.
Psalm 118:1

* * *

Story #19   Jesus Washes His Disciples' Feet

Jesus knew his hour had come. He understood human nature. Rather than begrudge the impending failures of his disciples, Jesus wants them to remember his teachings and his love for them. If you are in a setting where you can take off your shoes and socks, do so now. Imagine you are the disciple Peter. Prepare yourself, for your Lord is about to show his love for you. Use your senses to experience the cleansing and serving hands of Christ.

Take a moment to relax. Pray to be led by the Holy Spirit, and then enter into the story.

See – Listen – Taste – Smell – Touch

John 13:1–17

Now before the festival of the Passover, Jesus knew that his hour had come to depart from this world and go to the Father. Having loved his own who were in the world, he loved them to the end. The devil had already put it into the heart of Judas son of Simon Iscariot to betray him.

Customarily, the last days of the month of Nisan (March) are your favorite time of year. The warming breezes from the south persuade you that all is well in the world. As usual, the morning sun greeted you with affection and the day was full of excitement and preparations. After all, it's festival time. The flurry of activity in the city declares that the Passover celebration has reached its climax. Now, as the sun abandons the sky, a chill returns and darkness descends.

Yet, this year's Passover feels different. There's a knot in your stomach rather than a fire. You pull the hood of your cloak over your head to hide from a wind burst as you carry four loaves of bread to your rented room. *This week should be rich with a growing understanding of God, but instead, there's something unclean about it—a sense of unrest, an absence of delight in the air. It must be that my schedule has been so hectic. I haven't had enough time to pray. Even Jesus seems a little distant, not unsociable, preoccupied. And when he looks at me. . .I feel guilty, and I don't know why.*

And during supper Jesus, knowing that the Father had given all things into his hands, and that he had come from God and was going to God, got up from the table, took off his outer robe, and tied a towel around himself. Then he poured water into a basin and began to wash the disciples' feet and to wipe them with the towel that was tied around him.

Reclining at the table, you tap your chalice with the ring on your hand to get everyone's attention. And then you exclaim, "The women have outdone themselves again. If only I could collect the flavors and aromas of this meal—the bread, the roasted lamb—and bottle them for later, I'd be a contented man." A few cups of wine were emptied and many intoxicating stories of God's goodness to Israel were told this evening. You've told a few stories of your own, embellished in ways only you are capable of. You've seen God's activity in quite a few places recently.

Lying on his side, Jesus scans the room intently as if trying to store a special memory of each person. His gaze penetrates their skin and sees into their hearts. He knows their inner desires and motivations. *He knows us more completely than we know ourselves.* . . . His eyes meet your eyes. His scrutiny cuts through your pretense. *Yes, I may appear outgoing and extroverted to most, but they don't know the insecurity within that drives my exuberance.* His gaze is strangely warm yet uncomfortable. Quickly, you look away and ask James if he wants to join you when you go to the lake tomorrow.

Jesus stands up and all eyes follow him. He removes his outer cloak and the loose shirt underneath. The brawny muscles in his legs ripple. Climbing hills and mountainsides builds strength. The width of his shoulders makes him look strong like a ram. His torso is solid and unblemished.

He wraps a towel around his waist and fills a washbowl with water that has been warming on the oven. He walks over and places the basin next to your brother, Andrew. You cast a questioning glance at Thomas who reclines on the other side of the table as if to ask, "What's going on?" You whisper to James on your left, "He's our Master, not a servant. This isn't right."

He came to Simon Peter, who said to him, "Lord, are you going to wash my feet?" Jesus answered, "You do not know now what I am doing, but later you will understand." Peter said to him, "You will never wash my feet." Jesus answered, "Unless I wash you, you have no share with me." Simon Peter said to him, "Lord, not my feet only but also my hands and my head!" Jesus said to him, "One who has bathed does not need to wash, except for the feet, but is entirely clean. And you are clean, though not all of you." For he knew who was to betray him; for this reason he said, "Not all of you are clean."

Through the stairwell and windows of the room, music and laughter invade the stunned mood of your room. Traditions, celebrations, festive dinners continue unabated. Your heart pounds like a drum and rises to your throat as Jesus finishes with Andrew. *I hope he goes the other way so I have more time to understand this—and come up with a plan to stop it. This is embarrassing! What will people think?* Jesus pushes the basin of water toward you. It scrapes the floor and water sloshes dangerously close to its edges. "No, Jesus, don't do this. Not me. I can wash my own feet."

"No, Peter. . . . You cannot wash your own feet. I know you don't understand this, but trust me. Submit, even though you don't know why I must do this, and allow me to wash you. This is how it is to be done. And without it, you cannot follow me."

Reluctantly, you lower your eyes—*this is so uncomfortable*—yet you swing one foot in his direction.

He grasps your leg at the top of your calf with one hand and behind your ankle with the other. Strangely gentle, like a mare nudging her foal. Strangely soothing, like ointment in an open wound. There is no hint of forcefulness, no harshness, no attempt to show dominance. Jesus squeezes warm, cleansing water from a sponge over the top of your foot. Warm water spills down your foot and washes away grit from the dirt packed streets. Your muscles relax. The tension of life eases. Carefully, he lifts your foot so the water can flood between your toes and rinse the underside of your foot. Then taking a towel, he dries your foot. Let him repeat the process with your other foot.

As he moves to the next disciple, you say, "Wait, Jesus. I want more: cleanse my hands, cleanse my head."

He smiles. "Peter, you have already been prepared. It is only your feet that require constant washing. They alone come into contact with the dirt of the world. Just focus on keeping your feet clean. Yet there are some in here who are not bathed at all. They may appear clean, but the foul odor under their garments gives them away."

Jesus finishes the last person in the room. He puts on his outer garments and returns to the table. It's taken a long time, but you have learned to wait for his explanations. *His words feed me. I will meditate on what he asks me to do.*

After he had washed their feet, had put on his robe, and had returned to the table, he said to them, "Do you know what I have done to you? You call me Teacher and Lord—and you are right, for that is what I am. So if I, your Lord and Teacher, have washed *your feet, you also ought to wash one another's feet. For I have set you an example, that you also should do as I have done to you. Very truly, I tell you, servants are not greater than their master, nor are messengers greater than the one who sent them. If you know these things, you are blessed if you do them.*

* * *

Given that the fullness of God was shown in Jesus, visualize the story again but this time replace the name *Jesus* with a name for God that helps you imagine the Father/Creator in his place. Names to insert might be *Love*, *Goodness*, *Creator*, the *Breath of Life*, or come up with your own. Let this new encounter enrich your understanding of the nature and character of the Creator God.

When you are finished, reflect on how imagining the Creator in Jesus's place influences your understanding of God.

* * *

*Beloved, let us love one another,
because love is from God;
everyone who loves
is born of God and knows God.*
1 John 4:7

* * *

Story #20 The Birth of Jesus

This story may seem out of sequence. You've been imagining Jesus as an adult, in a relatively chronological progression of his ministry. But this is the story of his birth. Why? I have intentionally placed it before the stories leading to his death on the cross because Jesus came for a unique purpose. This story reveals the character of our God.

The baby Jesus is born to a common woman in the little town of Bethlehem. His life will not be filled with earthly comforts. He will be rejected and die, innocent of wrongdoing, at the hands of people who will accuse him of heresy (claiming he is under the influence of the ruler of demons) and will nail him to a cross like a criminal. Imagine yourself as Mary, the teenage mother of Jesus.

Take a moment to relax. Pray to be led by the Holy Spirit, and then enter into the story.

See – Listen – Taste – Smell – Touch

Luke 2:1–7

In those days a decree went out from Emperor Augustus that all the world should be registered. This was the first registration and was taken while Quirinius was governor of Syria. All went to their own towns to be registered. Joseph also went from the town of Nazareth in Galilee to Judea, to the city of David called Bethlehem, because he was descended from the house and family of David. He went to be registered with Mary, to whom he was engaged and who was expecting a child.

"Oh, Joseph, why now? Why must we travel so far, especially now? I don't know if I can walk ten miles a day. At that rate, it will take a week to reach Bethlehem. And I'm so big. It's hard enough to go to the well for water here in Nazareth."

Packing supplies into a coarse bag, he answers, "We will stop often. There's no hurry."

"I'm so concerned about the baby. What if I go into labor before we get there? What would we do?"

"Babies are born everywhere. We'll find a suitable place."

"Why would Rome require this of us? Do you think we could wait until after the baby is born? The angel said this child is so very special. I've tried to be careful and protective. And yet, I can only entrust the child to our God. . .and pray for the best."

"Mary, all will be well. I'm going to Josiah's to get the burro he said we could use to carry the supplies. Then we'll be ready to go."

You pack some bread and dried fish into a woven basket and cover them with a tightly knit yellow cloth made by your grandmother. When that runs out, someone will help. Being pregnant does have some advantages. The women in the villages you pass through will empathize. You won't go hungry.

The morning sun feels good as you and Joseph wave good-bye to family and friends. Oh! A sharp pain slices through your lower back. "Lord, have mercy."

After six days of travel: "Joseph, don't ever make me do this again! My legs and back feel like wet laundry being wrung dry." Your ankles are swollen to twice their normal size. "I feel like I carried the donkey rather than it carrying me. Please, Joseph, just find a soft place to rest."

While they were there, the time came for her to deliver her child. And she gave birth to her firstborn son and wrapped him in bands of cloth, and laid him in a manger, because there was no place for them in the inn.

Joseph's face is flushed as he exits the local inn. "I'm sorry, Mary; it's full." Tsunami-like contractions rise and fall within your abdomen. Muscles instinctively heave to expel an inhabitant who resists letting go of the comforts of his home. "The only place available to sleep is a stable in a local cave." People cackle from within the inn, laughing and swapping stories with childhood friends. "The innkeeper said we could stay in the stable. At least you will have a roof over your head."

"Oh, Joseph, hurry!"

With supercharged hormones taking over your senses, you can smell every odor that fills the stable: hay, straw, animals, mud. Another contraction swells and your eyes roll skyward, sweat dripping from your temples. Joseph hustles as he gathers straw for bedding. He throws it into a secluded stall and hurriedly spreads a blanket over it.

"Oh!" Knife-like pain causes you to gasp. *Why is giving birth so painful? Why is new life entering into the world so intense? Why did you do this to me, Lord?*

Joseph helps you remove your traveling garments. The sheep in the stable are bawling like little children. They're hungry. They seem to be saying, "Feed us." The old mare in the neighboring stall bows her head as if she knows this will be a long, difficult night, and closes her eyes as if to pray and give thanks for the honor of becoming a witness to the Gift.

A cool breath of wind caresses your forehead. "Thank you, Joseph. Is there any water? Did you. . . . Ooh! Help me. I feel him moving."

Pushing and pushing. . . . A new life breaks into the world. You know the night air hits his flesh like icy water splashing from a bucket. "Joseph, cover the baby." You hear him gasp and suck in his first taste of cold air. Expelled from the soft warmth of your protective womb, he exchanges paradise for a lost and needy world. It's dark and cold; the stable stinks. Yet a flicker of Light enters the darkness.

Joseph tenderly places the Anointed One in your arms. Holding him close to your heart, you gently wipe the blood and amniotic fluid from his velvet-soft skin. His little body radiates a surprising warmth. Such a sweet aroma from his little hands, these will touch and heal so many. His eyes are closed. Trace them with your finger, then his nose, his ear. Share the warmth of your body with him. Hear his uncomfortable cry. He's helpless, totally dependent on you to care for his needs—a precious gift of the living God. Sing a lullaby to him to assure him that he is loved. He will always be part of you. Nothing can take that away. The sounds of the stable drift away as you sink briefly into sleep.

A stirring in your arms startles you to wakefulness. Joseph gives you some soft cloths, and you wrap them around Jesus. "Here, take the baby and place him in one of the feeding troughs. Be careful!" You need more time to recover from the exhausting work. . .and to think about all that has happened. The visit from God's messenger. An unexpected, miraculous conception. What lies ahead for this special child? *Why did God chose me? What will be required of me? Whatever it is, I will do it.*

* * *

Given that the fullness of God was shown in Jesus, visualize the story again but this time replace the name *Jesus* with a name for God that helps you imagine the Father/Creator in his place. Names to insert might be *Love, Goodness, Creator,* the *Breath of Life,* or come up with your

own. Let this new encounter enrich your understanding of the nature and character of the Creator God.

When you are finished, reflect on how imagining the Creator in Jesus's place influences your understanding of God.

O TASTE AND SEE

* * *

Without any doubt,
the mystery of our religion is great:
He was revealed in flesh, vindicated in spirit,
seen by angels, proclaimed among Gentiles,
believed in throughout the world,
taken up in glory.
1 Timothy 3:16

* * *

Story #21 The Lord's Supper

In this story, Jesus encourages his disciples to remember him when they gather together to eat and drink. They promise to be faithful to him and his teachings. Use your eyes, hands, ears, nose, and tongue to participate in this last meal with the man you have been following for three years. Participate in the place of Judas Iscariot.

Take a moment to relax. Pray to be led by the Holy Spirit, and then enter into the story.

See – Listen – Taste – Smell – Touch

Matthew 26:17–35

On the first day of Unleavened Bread the disciples came to Jesus, saying, "Where do you want us to make the preparations for you to eat the Passover?" He said, "Go into the city to a certain man, and say to him, 'The Teacher says, my time is near; I will keep the Passover at your house with my disciples.'" So the disciples did as Jesus had directed them, and they prepared the Passover meal.

Jerusalem bustles with excitement as people arrive in the holy city, filling it with the clatter of horses' hooves, bawling sheep, rattling wagons filled with goods to be sold. . . . Musicians cast a joyous spell on the streets with flutes and lyres. Dutifully, people arrive to fulfill their religious obligation. Many wear new garments—bright, colorful, and clean. The aromas of seasoned foods waft through the passageways. You enjoy this time of year. Bartering and trading comes easily for you, and there's a man you want to see about selling some goods for you in one of the booths. "Jesus, I'll be glad to be part of the group that goes in advance to help get things ready for the celebration."

"Okay, Judas."

You and three disciples hurry into the city and, as luck would have it, the room near the market is vacant. "Brothers, there some business I need to attend to. If you will sweep and prepare the room, I'll pick up the food as I walk through the marketplace." Slipping out the door, you head toward the temple. *It's time to take matters into my own hands and get this city moving in the right direction. The people won't tolerate seeing Jesus arrested....*

When it was evening, [Jesus] took his place with the twelve; and while they were eating, he said, "Truly I tell you, one of you will betray me." And they became greatly distressed and began to say to him one after another, "Surely not I, Lord?" He answered, "The one who has dipped his hand into the bowl with me will betray me. The Son of Man goes as it is written of him, but woe to that one by whom the Son of Man is betrayed! It would have been better for that one not to have been born." Judas, who betrayed him, said, "Surely not I, Rabbi?" He replied, "You have said so."

You hurry back to the room moments before Jesus and the rest of the disciples arrive. The three who have done the work bark their disapproval at your lengthy absence. *They'll just have to get over it. They'll thank me later.* Jesus, with the others, knocks on the doorframe to announce his arrival. You escape your annoyed friends by running to greet the newcomers and helping them remove their outer garments. They laugh and tell you about people they saw from their hometowns today. You scurry around the table, placing cups and plates in front of them. Bowls with matzo (a flatbread), karpas (parsley-like greens), charoset (a mixture of chopped nuts, apples, cinnamon, and wine), maror (bitter horseradish), and Pesach (roasted lamb) are set in place. All is ready.

Jesus opens with prayer. "Blessed are you, O Lord our God, ruler of the universe, for you kept us alive and sustained us and brought us to this season." He leads you in the hand washing ceremony: "Blessed are you, O Lord our God, ruler of the universe, for you have blessed us with your commandments that we might serve you with pure and holy hands." Together you dip your fingers into the water bowl provided for cleansing.

In spite of the festivity during the meal, Jesus stops the mood in its tracks. With shocking directness, he says, "One of you is going to betray me." *Betray you? Who would do that? Once my plan succeeds, I'll help you find out who the traitor is!* Without exception, each of your friends around the table responds incredulously, "Surely you don't think I would do that, my Lord!" "Not me, Jesus!" "I would never betray you."

Dipping your fingers into the bowl of water at the same time Jesus dips his own, you are the last to speak, "Surely, Jesus, you don't think I could do anything so terrible?"

"You have said so."

Pulling your hand away and wiping it with a cloth, you avoid his eyes, turn to James and say, "What's he talking about?"

> *While they were eating, Jesus took a loaf of bread, and after blessing it he broke it, gave it to the disciples, and said, "Take, eat; this is my body." Then he took a cup, and after giving thanks he gave it to them, saying, "Drink from it, all of you; for this is my blood of the covenant, which is poured out for many for the forgiveness of sins. I tell you, I will never again drink of this fruit of the vine until that day when I drink it new with you in my Father's kingdom."*

Peter says, "Jesus, you are always talking in images and riddles—the light of the world, the vine, the way, the truth. Now, finally, you give a concrete image I can see and touch. Flat bread has not been influenced by yeast. I get this one. You have no malice, and if I take you into me and you become part of me. . .then maybe I'll become more like you, my teacher." Reaching out his hand, Peter says, "Thank you, I'll have some of that bread."

Peter, you think you know everything. You just wait until you see what I'm setting up. You'll admit it's brilliant.

Andrew receives the cup filled with wine and says, "Blood? Of course, this is the Passover meal in which we remember how God freed our ancestors from slavery to Pharaoh in Egypt. The blood of a lamb was painted over the doorways of the chosen people, Israel, so they would be protected from the angel of death, and God made a covenant with our people to protect them if they would follow the law. I know we're not doing a very good job with our part of the agreement, but we're human, you know."

Andrew drinks from the cup, while on the other side of Jesus, Matthew asks, "What do you mean your blood is poured out, Jesus? I've seen you forgive people their sins, but this is a little strange. You want us to drink your blood? Moses said we weren't supposed to drink the blood of any living thing; it's the life force. You're losing me, Jesus, but I don't mind that you fill my cup with wine again."

Matthew, don't read more into this than is necessary. Soon, you'll have more wine than you ever dreamed possible when we take over.

With visions of splendor, you address your rabbi, "Jesus, I'm going to enjoy the next time we feast together—right after you take over Jerusalem." *Which won't be long from now.* "I've seen enough to know you are the Messiah whom God promised long ago, and I have some ideas of my own about how to help God's kingdom to come a little more quickly. I've been thinking about this a lot."

When they had sung the hymn, they went out to the Mount of Olives.
Then Jesus said to them, "You will all become deserters because of me this night; for it is written,

*'I will strike the shepherd,
and the sheep of the flock will be scattered.'
But after I am raised up, I will go ahead of you to Galilee."
Peter said to him, "Though all become deserters because of you, I will never desert you." Jesus said to him, "Truly I tell you, this very night, before the cock crows, you will deny me three times." Peter said to him, "Even though I must die with you, I will not deny you." And so said all the disciples.*

After the closing hymn, you put on your cloak and, with the others, follow Jesus to the Mount of Olives. It's a cold night and there's more activity on the streets than normal. Upon arriving, Jesus turns and says, "All of you will desert me. This is what the ancient writings have said."

Peter gasps, "Jesus! How can you say we will desert you? We've followed you for three years! We have all declared our loyalty to you. You are our teacher, our Lord. We will follow you through wind, rain, storms, and wildernesses. We will even lay down our lives for you. Don't insult us."

You add, "We have made a public profession of our undying faith. We will serve you and help you when become king over Israel."

Thaddeus, who rarely speaks, says, "Not so, Jesus. We will *never* deny you!"

You tap Andrew on the shoulder and say, "I've got some business to attend to briefly in Jerusalem. I won't be gone long."

* * *

Bearing in mind that the fullness of the Godhead is shown in Jesus, place the Creator into the person of Jesus and experience the story again. Let this encounter enrich your understanding of the nature and character of the Creator.

When you are finished, reflect on how imagining the Creator in Jesus's place impacts your understanding of God.

* * *

*Jesus said to them,
"Very truly, I tell you,
before Abraham was,
I am."*
John 8:58

* * *

Story #22   Jesus Anointed in Bethany

What has happened immediately prior to a story and what happens after it often add to the meaning of the story. In the verses before this story, the chief priests and scribes are plotting how they might capture Jesus and put him to death. The verses that follow reveal how the plot is fulfilled: Judas Iscariot agrees to betray Jesus. Keep this in mind as you experience the story.

As much as Jesus taught that we should help the poor, widows and orphans, the hungry, the naked, etc., this story seems a little out of character for Jesus. What is he saying? Imagine yourself as the woman who anoints Jesus. What are the motivations for her actions that make this contribution acceptable to him?

Take a moment to relax. Pray to be led by the Holy Spirit, and then enter into the story.

See – Listen – Taste – Smell – Touch

Mark 14:3–9

While [Jesus] *was at Bethany in the house of Simon the leper, as he sat at the table, a woman came with an alabaster jar of very costly ointment of nard, and she broke open the jar and poured the ointment on his head.*

Your neighbor, Ruth, comes running to your door and shouts, "Jesus of Nazareth is in the village! He's at Simon's house!"

You know Jesus personally.[7] He's a good man. Wise, compassionate and caring—although a little too radical for some people. You met him when your brother, Lazarus invited him into your home.[8] His comments captivated you, and he affirmed you when you chose to listen to his teaching instead of abiding by the expectations of others. More significant, he brought your brother back to life after having been in the tomb four days. God is with this man.

Now, the gossip around town is that the religious leaders want him out of the way. The other day when Thomas the Baker mentioned his name, their faces got flushed and they gritted their teeth. They don't need to say much, their body language says it all. Everyone knows that anyone who bucks the system doesn't last long.

And now Jesus is at Simon's house. Simon is a decent man even though it's common knowledge he had leprosy two years ago. It's hard to shake the labels people place on others. During that time, he was denied participation in the synagogue. Stay away from lepers, they said. He never returned to the synagogue, even after Jesus healed him. Yet he took in Sara's boy after she died.

I wonder why Jesus stopped there. Is he trying to help Simon's reputation, or was it by invitation? Simon has done a good job at hiding the scars from the disease so others aren't afraid of any continuing impurity. It could be that Jesus is safer right now in a former leper's house than in a religious leader's house!

Hurrying, you reach behind the mat you sleep on and retrieve a small alabaster flask of nard. Your mother gave it to you a week before she died. Circumstances didn't allow you to use it. But not in a million years would you sell it. Never. All that is your past, all that is valuable to you, is in this flask. It would be like selling the last memory of your mother and grandmother and all the family tradition that has made you who you are today.

Gripping the flask to your heart, you dash out the open doorway and sprint around the corner to Simon's. *I hope Jesus hasn't left.* The sound of your sandals slapping the heels of your feet causes villagers along the path to look at you. Hastily, they back out of your way. *Good. There are people still standing in Simon's doorway.* A couple of Pharisees linger, mumbling to each other, on the other side of the road. Gasping for air, you halt behind the people staring into the entry of Simon's house. Why don't they go in? *No one's going to stop me from reaching Jesus.*

Once inside, you approach Jesus. He's reclining at the table and facing away from you. *I'm tired of proper protocols. He opened my eyes to what's important. I'm done worrying about what others might be thinking.* Propped up on one arm, Jesus reaches for a piece of warm bread. Lowering your eyes, you drop to your knees behind him. You reach out and touch his shoulder to make him aware of your presence. He continues listening to Simon across the table, and a soft smile creases his lips. *It's almost like he's been waiting for me. . .and it's like no one else is in the room. He places no restrictions on me, a woman, in a public setting.*

Taking an iron tent spike from your pocket, you shatter the neck of the flask. A powerful aroma of nard permeates the room. You begin to pour the liquid; it's all that you own, all that is you. The dense liquid streams smoothly from the bottle onto his head. With your fingers, you stroke it into his glistening hair. His hair—thick and dark—glistens as the oily perfume seeps to his scalp. Never have you experienced such a sensitive human being. *I will. . .I will give my life for you, Lord.*

A voice inside you asks, "How can I be doing this?" You reply, "How can I not do this?" Softly and slowly massage the ointment with both hands around his head, over his ears, along his cheeks and neck. *How near he is to me. He trusts me to come near and touch him.* All that was stored in that flask is now given over and absorbed into him.

> But some were there who said to one another in anger, "Why was the ointment wasted in this way? For this ointment could have been sold for more than three hundred denarii, and the money given to the poor." And they scolded her.

"What are you doing, woman?! How can you afford to squander what is of such great value like that? Don't you realize how much good you could do for those who need the basic necessities of life? You could help a lot of poor people if you sold it. Jesus is a fine man, but that's a lot of money! How can you be so wasteful?"

But Jesus said, "Let her alone; why do you trouble her? She has performed a good service for me. For you always have the poor with you, and you can show kindness to them whenever you wish; but you will not always have me. She has done what she could; she has anointed my body beforehand for its burial. Truly I tell you, wherever the good news is proclaimed in the whole world, what she has done will be told in remembrance of her."

The need to defend yourself disappeared the day you heard his teaching. Jesus stands with you against the people of your own village. He accepts your precious gift with open arms. But what he says is curious: "The poor will always be here, but I won't. Be kind to the poor when I'm no longer here" and "The world will hear what you have done."

What does my gift have to do with Jesus's burial? I'm no fortune teller. Yes, the rumors made me fear that he might suddenly disappear. You did this to honor and thank him for the abundant life you have found because of him. . .and the gift of more time with your brother. The nard was of no value to anyone in its hiding place. You've only done what you could to show him your gratitude.

* * *

Given that the fullness of God was shown in Jesus, visualize the story again but this time replace the name *Jesus* with a name for God that helps you imagine the Father/Creator in his place. Names to insert might be *Love, Goodness, Creator,* the *Breath of Life,* or come up with your

own. Let this new encounter enrich your understanding of the nature and character of the Creator God.

When you are finished, reflect on how imagining the Creator in Jesus's place influences your understanding of God.

* * *

*I believe
that I shall see the goodness of the Lord
in the land of the living.*
Psalm 27:13

* * *

Story #23 Jesus in Gethsemane

The mind may be willing but the flesh is weak. Still, God is patient, accepting of the time it takes for the flesh to mature and catch up with one's desires. The date of the Passover feast falls in either March or April of each year. The temperatures are unpredictable. One day, it might be warm. The next day could be cold. As one of his disciples who attended the Passover meal, some questions linger in your mind. Jesus said some confusing things. Betrayer? The bread and wine are his body and blood? Do these things to remember him? Is he going somewhere soon? Jesus's teachings have often required some time to think about them. If he wants you to understand, he will explain. Go with Jesus now. He has asked you to keep him company while he prays in the garden.

Take a moment to relax. Pray to be led by the Holy Spirit, and then enter into the story.

See – Listen – Taste – Smell – Touch

Matthew 26:36–46

Then Jesus went with them to a place called Gethsemane; and he said to his disciples, "Sit here while I go over there and pray."

Filled! bodily and spiritually—the ceremony of the Passover often brings tears to your eyes. To hear again the story of how God brought Israel out of bondage in Egypt to the Promised Land. . . . God is so good! Through the meal, however, you noticed Jesus became increasingly grave. Uncharacteristically, he missed some of the comments made in jest as the evening progressed.

You and the other disciples told story after story about where you saw God in the last year. You've never laughed as hard as you did when Peter told his version of getting out of the boat in the middle of the lake. You sopped your plate with the bread until it sparkled. You couldn't bear another bite, even though you remember looking over at Jesus and seeing that some food remained on his plate. That was odd. You asked, "Jesus, do you plan to finish what's left on your plate? You can't let good food go to waste!" When he looked at you, you felt like a child repeating a family precept. His smile looked tired. It was no surprise to hear him say, "Let's walk to the garden. I need to pray." That will be a good way to end the evening.

Walking out the doorway of the room, you notice a chill has crept into the night air. You wrap your cloak around your shoulders and walk with Jesus up the slope to the garden. Laughter from houses in the city below wafts up the hillside as the meals in other households are coming to an end. Jesus picks up the pace as the path narrows.

"Wait, Jesus. . . . We've been reclining at the table for more than an hour. The food was excellent. The wine was plentiful. Is there more to do this evening? It's time to relax after the evening meal. Slow down."

> He took with him Peter and the two sons of Zebedee, and began to be grieved and agitated. Then he said to them, "I am deeply grieved, even to death; remain here, and stay awake with me."
> And going a little farther, he threw himself on the ground and prayed, "My Father, if it is possible, let this cup pass from me; yet not what I want but what you want."

You've come to Gethsemane often with him. Most of the time, you sit and visit with the other disciples at the entrance while he goes deeper into the garden. This time, he asks you and two others to follow him. So you leave the group. The path has gotten narrower, and darker. You've learned to be careful walking in the garden at dark. You don't get too close to the person ahead because a branch might come swinging back and hit you.

Walking a short distance, Jesus stops. He turns around and asks the three of you to stay in this place. "Pray for me. I'm deeply distressed."

"What's wrong, Jesus? Is this like the time you were standing on the hill, looking over Jerusalem? Remember how upset you were when you saw how much it was straying from God's will? We'll be going back to Galilee after the Sabbath and things will get back to normal."

Jesus walks into the darkness.

You look to find a place to sit down, and in a loud voice you ask, "How long will you be?" But there's no answer. The garden, which feels darker than usual, swallowed him quickly. You know this area well. He'll be okay. He always is.

Good, here's a nice tree you can lean against. Get settled for a short time of prayer. "Oh, yes, that was good wine tonight." Pull your cloak around your knees, making it like a tent. Tuck your head down and let your breath add warmth to the space inside.

> Then he came to the disciples and found them sleeping; and he said to Peter, "So, could you not stay awake with me one hour? Stay awake and pray that you may not come into the time of trial; the spirit indeed is willing, but the flesh is weak."

A voice from the darkness startles you. "Huh? Who's that? Jesus? Oh, I'm so sorry. I must have dozed off. It's been a long day, you know. . . . But I'll do better, I promise. You can count on me, Jesus. Prayer is one of my favorite things, and I can do this for you since I can see it's so important to you. I'll just sit up a little straighter against this tree and work harder at it."

Again he went away for the second time and prayed, "My Father, if this cannot pass unless I drink it, your will be done." Again he came and found them sleeping, for their eyes were heavy. So leaving them again, he went away and prayed for the third time, saying the same words.

The sweet music of a rising wind, like the breath of God, drifts through the leaves of the trees in the garden. Tiny lights sparkle in the heavens, waiting to be smothered by angry clouds stirring in the distance. A phrase mysteriously echoes in your mind as drift off again: *Your will be done...Your will be done....*

Then he came to the disciples and said to them, "Are you still sleeping and taking your rest? See, the hour is at hand, and the Son of Man is betrayed into the hands of sinners. Get up, let us be going. See, my betrayer is at hand."

Jesus places his hand on your shoulder. "What? Is it time to go already? I must have just dozed off. . . . I have been praying, really. It's just been a long day. What do you mean 'betrayer'? You said something about that earlier, during the meal. Jesus, you know I would never betray you nor let anyone else. I will always stand with you. You can count on me."

* * *

With the fullness of God shown in Jesus, visualize the story again but this time replace the name *Jesus* with a name for God that helps you imagine the Father/Creator in his place: *Love, Goodness, Creator,* the *Breath of Life,* or come up with your own. Let this new encounter enrich your understanding of the nature and character of the Creator God.

Reflect on how imagining the Creator in Jesus's place influences your understanding of God.

* * *

For since the creation of the world
His invisible attributes are clearly seen,
being understood by the things that are made,
even His eternal power and Godhead.
Romans 1:20 (NKJV)

* * *

Story #24 Jesus Arrested

Like a sudden storm on the Sea of Galilee, life changes with little warning. One moment all seems well. The next, chaos reigns. Fiery torches of anger and injustice break through the darkness, chasing away any sense of peace from an evening's end. The world gets in your face without warning, with no respect for your personal space.

Has injustice burst into your life recently? Has your space been invaded by those who don't care what your good intentions might be? Become one of the disciples who followed Jesus into the garden and observe: How did Jesus handle the chaos?

Take a moment to relax. Pray to be led by the Holy Spirit, and then enter into the story.

See – Listen – Taste – Smell – Touch

Matthew 26:47–56

While [Jesus] was still speaking, Judas, one of the twelve, arrived; with him was a large crowd with swords and clubs, from the chief priests and the elders of the people. Now the betrayer had given them a sign, saying, "The one I will kiss is the man; arrest him." At once he came up to Jesus and said, "Greetings, Rabbi!" and kissed him. Jesus said to him, "Friend, do what you are here to do."

Darkness thickens around the garden of Gethsemane and the stars have gone into hiding. You're still trying to get your bearings, having just wakened from sleep. Jesus says, "Get up; let us be going. See, my betrayer is at hand." Clumping feet and clanging metal startle you out of your post-dinner stupor. You scramble to your feet as the stillness of the night is attacked by a wild-eyed mob of temple guards and sanctimonious loyalists. Raucously, they stab the air with angry torches and thunderous threats of bodily harm. Their flames reek of tar and spew off an oily black smoke that has soiled the faces of the accusers. As they surround you, a careless flame behind you singes the hair on your neck. You turn quickly to face the threat while keeping your friends at your back.

A fellow disciple slithers through the crowd filled with assistants to the religious hierarchy. Judas speaks as if nothing is amiss. "Greetings, Teacher. It's a wonderful night for a walk in the garden."

Your stomach twists in knots. He walks up with a smile on his face and gives Jesus the usual sign of greeting, a kiss. Betrayed, in an embrace of false friendship and hypocrisy....

With no animosity in his eyes or voice, as if destiny was his partner, a solemn Jesus says, "Do what you have come to do...friend."

Then they came and laid hands on Jesus and arrested him. Suddenly, one of those with Jesus put his hand on his sword, drew it, and struck the slave of the high priest, cutting off his ear. Then Jesus said to him, "Put your sword back into its place; for all who take the sword will perish by the sword. Do you think that I cannot appeal to my Father, and he will at once send me more than twelve legions of angels? But how then would the scriptures be fulfilled, which say it must happen in this way?"

The guards, who don't know your gentle Lord, seize him as if he's a threat, as if he's a strong man possessed by an evil spirit. They strike him with wooden clubs, pulling at the arms that gave comfort and healing to so many sick and lonely people and twisting them behind his back. One grabs Jesus by the hair and yanks him in the direction toward the path.

This isn't right! You've never seen Jesus in hand-to-hand combat, but you can't let these temple loyalists destroy Jesus. You draw your sword to strike back. *I don't care if I hurt someone. I'm protecting my Lord.* No one treats the Son of God like this.

Gripping the handle with both hands, you swing the sword with all your might. Clashing with your opponent's sword raised in defense, your weapon bounces off and slices an ear from the high priest's assistant. Fully engaged in the conflict, another mob-crazed fanatic replaces him and you swing again. *Jesus is the way and I'll go to my death defending him.*

"What, Jesus? Stop fighting? Well, go ahead and call down your legions of angels. Can't you see we need them? Do it now! Are you all talk and no action?" Who wouldn't defend himself against evil? Obediently, you lower your weapon but hold it ready to defend yourself in case anyone else steps forward to attack.

At that hour Jesus said to the crowds, "Have you come out with swords and clubs to arrest me as though I were a bandit? Day after day I sat in the temple teaching, and you did not arrest me. But all this has taken place, so that the scriptures of the prophets may be fulfilled." Then all the disciples deserted him and fled.

Looking at the people who've come to arrest Jesus, you recognize the religious emblems hanging around their necks: symbols of ancient tradition, breastplates of laws and ordinances, adorned with jewels indicating rank and position, bloodied by the sacrifice of innocent creatures to an angry God. They justify their defense of Mosaic law. They fear God will lose this battle against revolutionaries to the faith and evil. They must destroy any threat to the ground they've stood on for centuries.

You decide that your small force of twelve is no match against a thousand years of tradition. The crowd of temple guards grows only larger. The swords upholding religious law and ritual are too powerful. It's no use to stand with the Son of God against all that is seeking to do away with him. And so, you drop your sword and flee into the darkness, tripping on roots of primeval trees that firmly grip the stones of earth, raising your arms in front of you to block the branches that slap your face...and leave the Fulfillment of the Promise himself to endure the ugliness of impending violence and pain. The Prince of Peace, Immanuel, the infant from the manger shackled in chains and man-handled as if he were the lowest of sinners.

And now, the image of Grace and Mercy stands alone, deserted by all who vowed they would follow him to their deaths.

* * *

Given that the fullness of God was shown in Jesus, visualize the story again but this time replace the name *Jesus* with a name for God that helps you imagine the Father/Creator in his place. Names to insert might be *Love*, *Goodness*, *Creator*, the *Breath of Life*, or come up with your own. Let this new encounter enrich your understanding of the nature and character of the Creator God.

When you are finished, reflect on how imagining the Creator in Jesus's place influences your understanding of God.

* * *

*So we have known and believe
the love that God has for us.
God is love,
and those who abide in love abide in God,
and God abides in them.
1 John 4:16*

* * *

Story #25   Jesus before the Sanhedrin

The penalty for breaking certain statutes of the Law of Moses was death: blasphemy, adultery, cursing one's parents, working on the Sabbath, and sorcery. This sounds harsh, but the stated purpose was to eradicate sin from the community "so that no wickedness will be among you" (Lev. 20:14). Centuries after Moses handed down the law, killing people for these actions was not universally enforced. How could a nation survive if the penalties for such laws were mandatory? Yet these laws were still considered the word of God.

As you meditate on this story, consider how Jesus's actions shook the religious establishment to its core. He openly opposed the most popular interpretations of decrees from Moses. He added new commands. Jesus deliberately deviated from the religious practices of over one thousand years. And in quiet acceptance, he understood how human nature would react to change of this magnitude. Imagine yourself as Peter, the only disciple reported to have gained access to the inner courtyard where Jesus stood before the religious council.

Take a moment to relax. Pray to be led by the Holy Spirit, and then enter into the story.

See – Listen – Taste – Smell – Touch

Mark 14:53–65

They took Jesus to the high priest; and all the chief priests, the elders, and the scribes were assembled. Peter had followed him at a distance, right into the courtyard of the high priest; and he was sitting with the guards, warming himself at the fire.

Breathing heavily, you glance back to insure no one is following you and then duck behind two scraggly shrubs. Sweat drips down your neck and your cheek stings from meeting the rough bark of an olive tree. A streak of blood memorializes the event. You need time to collect your thoughts. Too much is happening too fast. Thumping like a drum, your heart tells you to go back, see what is happening to Jesus. Peering through the scrub brush, you see no one has bothered to search for you. You crawl onto your knees, stand, and creep back to get closer to the center of activity around Jesus.

Now, two men grab Jesus and hold his arms down while another ties a rope around his arms and torso. They begin to push him toward Jerusalem, the city of peace. The stench of tar from their torches fades, along with the sound of metal clanking on metal. Distantly, they laugh with satisfaction at the success of their mission. Darkness grows as the Light disappears in the hands of the religious authorities. As you stand, you notice more blood on your hands and knees. Pushing branches aside, you step onto the narrow path and stumble like a drunk man down to the gate where you suspect they are taking Jesus. You need to know what's going to happen.

Closer to the gate that opens into the courtyard, you join four jovial warriors for the God of Abraham. They stop at a local wine seller and pick up another bottle of courage. You need to blend in, so you buy a bottle too, a small bottle. The night has turned bitter and an icy wind cuts through your cloak. The cozy meal in the upper room a few hours ago has vanished as cold water now splashes on your dreams for the new kingdom that you envisioned.

Sliding quietly inside the gate, you quickly move to stand close to the fire. The flames only seem to uncover the depth of coldness within the courtyard. The quivering light exposes irritation in the faces of those who guard the temple; they act as if their eternal fate rests on the temple remaining unchanged.

Now the chief priests and the whole council were looking for testimony against Jesus to put him to death; but they found none.

For many gave false testimony against him, and their testimony did not agree. Some stood up and gave false testimony against him, saying, "We heard him say, 'I will destroy this temple that is made with hands, and in three days I will build another, not made with hands.'" But even on this point their testimony did not agree.

Jesus stands at the foot of the steps in the courtyard while the religious leaders perform a mock trial to make their actions appear ethical. The temple guard next to you slips a coin to a man in front of him. He says, "Go tell them that Jesus has been meeting in secret with people. Tell them he says they can work on the Sabbath." Another person steps forward and says, "It is written in the Scripture that adulterers should be put to death. This false teacher says a person commits adultery if you merely think about having intercourse with someone. He suggests we should kill people for their thoughts! How absurd!" People around you laugh hysterically. You turn to the guard and laugh too, otherwise you won't blend in.

Then the high priest stood up before them and asked Jesus, "Have you no answer? What is it that they testify against you?" But he was silent and did not answer.

Jesus stands like a rock in a raging river. Is this man you've been following a fool? Nobody lets people accuse them without fighting back. Yet why fight against conflicting accusations? One vows that Jesus said he would destroy the temple and rebuild it with no hands. Another stands and screeches, "I heard Jesus say no stone would be left on another, the temple would be torn apart, stone by stone. He said nothing about rebuilding anything."

If he keeps quiet, his silence can't condemn him. . . in silence, the world began.

Again the high priest asked him, "Are you the Messiah, the Son of the Blessed One?" Jesus said, "I am; and
    'you will see the Son of Man

*seated at the right hand of the Power,'
and 'coming with the clouds of heaven.'"*

Oh no, Jesus, why did you say that? You steal a glance at the widening grin on the temple guard's face. *You just fell into their trap and sealed your fate.* "Yes, I am the Messiah. And one day, your own eyes will be opened to that fact." *Keeping your mouth shut was in your best interest, Jesus. Now all hell is going to break loose! Why did you make these claims in front of people who are looking for any reason to accuse you? Don't you care about yourself?*

Then the high priest tore his clothes and said, "Why do we still need witnesses? You have heard his blasphemy! What is your decision?" All of them condemned him as deserving death. Some began to spit on him, to blindfold him, and to strike him, saying to him, "Prophesy!" The guards also took him over and beat him.

With a gasp and a spectacle certain to raise the ire of onlookers, the high priest clutches his garment with both hands, violently tears the fabric, and then bellows, "Unbelievable! He commits blasphemy right in front of us. Moses has told us how to deal with blasphemers. What do you say?"

"Death. It's the law." "Yes, it's the law!"

Jesus, why did you say what you said? Emptied of hope that there might be a way out for your rabbi, you slide behind a tall column and sink deep into its shadow. *But is it a good law if it doesn't promote love? God is goodness and love!*

No longer in control of their actions, they intensify the cruelty heaped upon the only man who followed the law as a guide to loving God and his neighbor. With fists of rage, they strike the Good Shepherd. Others spew vulgarities and launch biblical arrows to wreak shame on the gentle healer you've been following for three years.

How can they do this? What are they so afraid of? Tears run down your cheeks. *How is beating this good man upholding God's honor?*

Jesus raises his head after every blow, blood blowing from his mouth and brow, while bruises multiply across his body. He returns no insults, no evil. The kingdom of heaven is near to him.

* * *

Given that the fullness of God was shown in Jesus, visualize the story again but this time replace the name *Jesus* with a name for God that helps you imagine the Father/Creator in his place. Names to insert might be *Love*, *Goodness*, *Creator*, the *Breath of Life*, or come up with your own. Let this new encounter enrich your understanding of the nature and character of the Creator God.

When you are finished, reflect on how imagining the Creator in Jesus's place influences your understanding of God.

* * *

*They shall celebrate
the fame of your abundant goodness,
and shall sing aloud
of your righteousness.*
Psalm 145:7

* * *

Story #26   Jesus before Pilate

The stories in the Gospels hold many layers of teachings, depending on which viewpoint you choose. The next two meditations will use the same biblical text, but offer views from two different perspectives.

Many Christians remember Pilate's attempt to set Jesus free using the tradition of allowing one prisoner to go free during the Passover. This was an act of mercy displayed by a foreign, oppressive regime. Even human institutions are capable of showing mercy to those who don't deserve it. As you live inside this story, imagine yourself as Barabbas, condemned for violations against civil law.

Take a moment to relax. Pray to be led by the Holy Spirit, and then enter into the story.

See – Listen – Taste – Smell – Touch

Matthew 27:1–2, 11–26

When morning came, all the chief priests and the elders of the people conferred together against Jesus in order to bring about his death. They bound him, led him away, and handed him over to Pilate the governor. . . .
Now Jesus stood before the governor; and the governor asked him, "Are you the King of the Jews?" Jesus said, "You say so." But when he was accused by the chief priests and elders, he did not answer. Then Pilate said to him, "Do you not hear how many accusations they make against you?" But he gave him no answer, not even to a single charge, so that the governor was greatly amazed.

A hint of torchlight flickers through an opening to your tiny prison chamber beneath the earth. Your small compartment near the entrance of the jail is reserved for those soon to be executed. The stench of human excrement is overwhelming. You cup your hands and press your nose against a crack in the wall trying to get a breath of clean air from the outside.

In the darkness, a mixed chorus of pain, despair, and anger irritates any sleep that has tried to roost. It's a dismal place to spend your last hours. The Roman system permits no delays in handing out punishment. What little time lingers to think about what it feels like to hang on a cross drags like an eternity.

Sleep has never been a faithful friend. With a rock, you scratch an image on the ceiling as you lie in wait, like a mole in a narrow tunnel. One angry voice that bounces off the indifferent walls is your own: "You Romans have no right to tell me what to do! Get out of my country, you pigs!" Another prisoner cries out in fear and self-defense, "I didn't do it. I didn't do it. You've got to believe me. I have a family."

"Shut up," you scream. "I've got my own problems. I don't need yours too!"

A commotion outside the jail entry signals another trial is beginning in the courtyard. It's odd though, you've never heard of a trial being held at night. Someone doesn't want to be noticed. *Someone is evading the justice system again. Money can buy anything.* Thirty minutes crawl by. A guard walks by the opening to your cell and grumbles to another guard, "It's the Jews again. This time they want a Galilean rabbi crucified."

"Who is it?" you ask.

"Jesus of Nazareth."

The healer loved by the people? There were rumors circulating for months that some were out to get him, but that was of no concern to you. You avoided him like you avoided all rabbis you saw on the streets. You never wanted anyone tell you how to live your life. The people are bewitched by this Nazarene, but the scribes and Pharisees hate him. This religious stuff is a farce. Torturing a man is a godly kind of justice? What a joke!

Rusty chains on Jesus's feet scrape the hard flooring in the courtyard. Your own ankles sting as sweat drips across open blisters, raw and bloody from the loosely fitting iron shackles. *I don't know what's worse, these foot irons or the coarse ropes they use to tie your hands. Ropes and shackles are no different than religious rules used to make prisoners of every man and woman.*

A man shouts accusations against the Nazarene: "He breaks our laws. He healed a man on the Sabbath. He offends our God by allowing his followers to pick grain and eat it on the Sabbath." Another shrieks, "He blasphemes by saying he is God Himself. He threatens to destroy our temple. He makes claims that are preposterous." *But has he hurt anyone?* The pious authorities want this man silenced. How do they call this religious? You think back into your childhood, being told that God gave a law saying the punishment should never be greater than the crime...an eye for an eye. Why do the priests break that one? To kill a man when he didn't kill anyone? *What about the command of Moses not to kill?* You've seen their leaders pick and choose the rules that suit their views, never understanding it. So you stayed away from the hypocrisy.

You've been listening intently, but you've not heard any response from the accused. Most people vehemently deny doing anything wrong, even when they've been caught red-handed. This man is harmless, offers no resistance. His only threat is to buck tradition and the authority of the religious leadership. For this he will die?

Now at the festival the governor was accustomed to release a prisoner for the crowd, anyone whom they wanted. At that time they had a notorious prisoner, called Jesus Barabbas. So after they had gathered, Pilate said to them, "Whom do you want me to release for you, Jesus Barabbas or Jesus who is called the Messiah?" For he realized that it was out of jealousy that they had handed him over. While he was sitting on the judgment seat, his wife sent word to him, "Have nothing to do with that innocent man, for today I have suffered a great deal because of a dream about him."

Now the chief priests and the elders persuaded the crowds to ask for Barabbas and to have Jesus killed. The governor again said to them, "Which of the two do you want me to release for you?" And they said, "Barabbas." Pilate said to them, "Then what should I do with Jesus who is called the Messiah?" All of them said, "Let him be crucified!" Then he asked, "Why, what evil has he done?" But they shouted all the more, "Let him be crucified!"

Two prison guards approach the opening of your cell with their torches. One fumbles for a key in the dim light and unlocks the chain to your shackles. The mere sight of the open door offers hope, a momentary gust of freedom from this living tomb. You don't care if they curse you, embarrass you, beat you, or kill you. Just give you a breath of fresh air.

Pushed into the judgment arena, you stumble and fall against Jesus. His eyes meet your own with sadness and, of all things, mercy. Then you hear Pilate shout, "Who do you want set free this year? Jesus of Nazareth or Jesus Barabbas?" That's a joke. The people adore the healer. *They might as well get my cross ready.*

The servant of Pilate's wife runs into the room and whispers to Pilate. Yet he, in the heat of this emotional conflict, is preoccupied. "Who shall I set free? Jesus, who is called the Messiah, or Jesus Barabbas?"

"We want Barabbas!"

What? They want me to go free? The people say they want freedom for me? A rebel who lives only by my own rules? Maybe I'm not so bad. . . .

So when Pilate saw that he could do nothing, but rather that a riot was beginning, he took some water and washed his hands before the crowd, saying, "I am innocent of this man's blood; see to it yourselves." Then the people as a whole answered, "His blood be on us and on our children!" So he released Barabbas for them; and after flogging Jesus, he handed him over to be crucified.

Pilate shakes his head and motions for a bowl of water. A servant scrambles to his side and water splashes on the rock floor. Pilate rinses his hands and shakes the water off in disgust. "Not my responsibility." The crowd cries, "We know what we're doing! This is how we deal with evil!"

The chains fall to the stone floor behind you as a Roman soldier unlocks them. The prison guards drag Jesus unmercifully to the whipping post where they take turns, lash after lash, ripping the skin of his back and arms and neck and legs, spilling his blood while you walk through the courtyard gate to freedom.

* * *

Given that the fullness of God was shown in Jesus, visualize the story again but this time replace the name *Jesus* with a name for God that helps you imagine the Father/Creator in his place. Names to insert might be *Love*, *Goodness*, *Creator*, the *Breath of Life*, or come up with your own. Let this new encounter enrich your understanding of the nature and character of the Creator God.

When you are finished, reflect on how imagining the Creator in Jesus's place influences your understanding of God.

* * *

This is the message we have heard from him
and proclaim to you,
that God is light
and in him there is no darkness at all.
1 John 1:5

* * *

Story #27   Sentenced to be Crucified

Poets and writers have been trying to describe the Inconceivable since the beginning of time. To comprehend is to feel secure. But who can understand why bad things happen to good people in a beautiful world? Does the Creator who brings what is good also initiate the bad? Can the problems of life be reduced or eliminated using ceremonies of ritual and sacrifice?

Knowledge of the Unknown calls for something the human senses can see, touch, hear, smell, or taste. For God to become intelligible required the Formless to embody a form—Jesus of Nazareth.

Jesus said the Father was in him and he was in the Father. Keep your eyes, ears, hands, and senses on Jesus to determine how he shows you the nature of the Formless. Place yourself in Jesus's flesh and taste the truth about God.

Take a moment to relax. Pray to be led by the Holy Spirit, and then enter into the story.

See – Listen – Taste – Smell – Touch

John 19:1–16

Then Pilate took Jesus and had him flogged. And the soldiers wove a crown of thorns and put it on his head, and they dressed him in a purple robe. They kept coming up to him, saying, "Hail, King of the Jews!" and striking him on the face. Pilate went out again and said to them, "Look, I am bringing him out to you to let you know that I find no case against him."

You are already bruised from blows to your cheeks; now soldiers strap you to a whipping post. Your robe is jerked away to expose a bare back to the early morning air. Immediately, the sharp cracking sound of leather straps, embedded with glass slivers, slaps your right shoulder and tears into your flesh. Hot streaks of pain flash under your skin. Gasping at the depth it reaches, your taut muscles clutch the embedded fragments. Warm blood spurts from the new laceration as the muscular soldier yanks the straps free and winds up for another strike. Snap! More streaks of searing pain radiate from low on your back, and you try to expel the air in your lungs, but it won't come out. A chorus of sinister laughter connects you to the reality of the human heart. "Look at him jump!" they shout with glee.

My own people provoked this treatment. I offered only goodness to them. The whip cracks again, repeatedly, relentlessly. Humanity strikes its Creator. Ugliness violates the beautiful. Snap!

A man with thick gloves presses a crown of thorns onto your head. Needle-like punctures draw blood quickly, and everlasting life drips like tears flowing down the side of your nose and into your mouth. Bittersweet, the taste reminds you why endured this wilderness: that they might taste the substance of life. The purpose for which you came continues, even in this event. The Creator is revealed.

The soldiers, trained to destroy the bodies and spirits of their own species, drape a purple robe over your shoulders. "Isn't this how it's done? Shouldn't we throw a pig or a goat in the fire too? Isn't that how you people call on your god?"

Pilate, as representative of civil government tells the religious establishment, "We find no reason to kill your king. He doesn't appear hateful, vengeful, or hurtful to us. Why do you do this to one of your own? Why do you pressure me to get rid of him?"

So Jesus came out, wearing the crown of thorns and the purple robe. Pilate said to them, "Here is the man!" When the chief priests and the police saw him, they shouted, "Crucify him! Crucify him!" Pilate said to them, "Take him yourselves and crucify him; I find no case against him." The Jews answered him, "We have a law, and according to that law he ought to die because he has claimed to be the Son of God."

When the Roman soldiers mock the Israelites by draping a purple robe over your shoulders as the king of the Jews, a powder keg of outrage is ignited. "Crucify him! Get rid of this false messiah. He's no leader we've chosen."

Pilate, standing next to you, lifts his hands and says to the temple leaders, "Take him yourself and do what you want to him. Don't ask me to do your dirty work. I've seen nothing that validates your claims."

They shriek, "He breaks our laws. People have to have rules. He claims to be the Son of God and our law says that's punishable by death."

Now when Pilate heard this, he was more afraid than ever. He entered his headquarters again and asked Jesus, "Where are you from?" But Jesus gave him no answer. Pilate therefore said to him, "Do you refuse to speak to me? Do you not know that I have power to release you, and power to crucify you?" Jesus answered him, "You would have no power over me unless it had been given you from above; therefore the one who handed me over to you is guilty of a greater sin." From then on Pilate tried to release him, but the Jews cried out, "If you release this man, you are no friend of the emperor. Everyone who claims to be a king sets himself against the emperor."
When Pilate heard these words, he brought Jesus outside and sat on the judge's bench at a place called The Stone Pavement, or in Hebrew Gabbatha.

Pilate wipes his brow with a small towel, caught in a venomous predicament. He motions for a soldier to grab hold of you and follow him as he retreats to his headquarters. Passing through a doorway, he curses and flings his towel, striking a candleholder on a table and sends it clanging to the floor. "I don't care if these religious advocates think you are violating some unseen god. What's real is Caesar, and he can take my job if I let this go any further. Man, tell me, where are you from?"

It's hard to do the right thing, isn't it? Blood thickens on your eyelids; you lower your eyes and stare at the floor.

He stands inches away from your face and shouts, "Say something! Why won't you help me? Don't you realize I can let you go or have you crucified for these charges of claiming to be a son of the gods? Help me out here."

Your voice feeble, you answer. "You have less control in this matter than you think. But I will say this: the one who has handed me over to you is guilty of a greater wrong."

Pilate sits down at his table. "This isn't right," he mutters. After a moment, he gets up quickly and tramps out to the crowd. "I'm letting this man go."

One of the men in the front of the crowd yells, "You're no ally of the emperor if you release a man who claims to be a king and lives in this territory. He's got more people than you think who follow him."

Still tasting blood in your mouth, Pilate sits down on a stone bench, as powerless to change their locked minds as it would be to open a deaf man's ears. He lowers his head and shuts his eyes. A decision has to be made.

Now it was the day of Preparation for the Passover; and it was about noon. [Pilate] *said to the Jews, "Here is your King!" They cried out, "Away with him! Away with him! Crucify him!" Pilate asked them, "Shall I crucify your King?" The chief priests answered, "We have no king but the emperor." Then he handed him over to them to be crucified.*

Pilate stands and looks at the sun high in the sky. He shakes his head. He points a finger at you. In an empty plea, he reaches out his other hand toward the crowd, and says, "Here is your king!"

The Jews cry out, "No, no. He's no king of ours. He deserves death. We want him crucified. Yes, crucify him!"

"You can't be serious! This is getting out of hand. This is your king and you want him tortured? Have you no mercy?"

The religious leaders respond, "Governor, you know we can have no king of our own. The emperor is our king."

The piercing pain from your torn skin and abrasions merges with the rejection of Israel's spiritual leaders. You gasp for relief from the hatred that rips into your heart. *What have I done to deserve this treatment? Yet, I will not be swayed to act like them. I will not return insult for insult, nor evil with evil.*

"How can you reason with people like this?" Pilate mutters to his court aide. "Oh well, he's only a Jew. Let them have him."

The crowd roars its approval.

You hang your head. *The prophesies are being fulfilled. God, help me.*

* * *

Given that the fullness of God was shown in Jesus, visualize the story again but this time replace the name *Jesus* with a name for God that helps you imagine the Father/Creator in his place. Names to insert might be *Love*, *Goodness*, *Creator*, the *Breath of Life*, or come up with your own. Let this new encounter enrich your understanding of the nature and character of the Creator God.

When you are finished, reflect on how imagining the Creator in Jesus's place influences your understanding of God.

O TASTE AND SEE

* * *

We declare to you what was from the beginning,
what we have heard,
what we have seen with our eyes,
what we have looked at
and touched with our hands,
concerning the word of life—
this life was revealed, and we have seen it
and testify to it, and declare to you
the eternal life that was with the Father
and was revealed to us.
1 John 1:1-2

* * *

Story #28   Jesus Cares for His Mother

In this story, Jesus asks his disciple to care for his mother. He thinks about her needs as he himself suffers wrenching pain on the cross. The New Testament says Jesus had brothers and sisters. Whether they were biological siblings or not, it's curious that Jesus asks a non-family member to take charge in caring for his mother instead of entrusting her to others in the family.

In this meditation, enter into the battered body of Jesus and experience the story from his viewpoint.

Take a moment to relax. Pray to be led by the Holy Spirit, and then enter into the story.

See – Listen – Taste – Smell – Touch

John 19:23–27

When the soldiers had crucified Jesus, they took his clothes and divided them into four parts, one for each soldier. They also took his tunic; now the tunic was seamless, woven in one piece from the top. So they said to one another, "Let us not tear it, but cast lots for it to see who will get it." This was to fulfill what the scripture says,
"They divided my clothes among themselves,
and for my clothing they cast lots."
And that is what the soldiers did.

Bolts of pain, like lightning, rocket from your wrists through your shoulder joints. The nails penetrate deeper than your flesh. They go straight into the heart. *What did I do that offended them so deeply?* Your thighs cramp as you push to raise your chest enough to gasp for a breath of air. Not because you want to breathe, but because your lungs demand it. Each gasp stokes the inferno rising from your feet and spreading through your back. Yet human bodies are designed to fight to survive in spite of what agony they encounter.

With shoulders torn out of joint, your body sags like it has tripled in weight, hanging like a millstone on the nails in your wrists. To utter any sound only intensifies the torture because then you must take another breath. The muscles in your diaphragm throb from trying to hold each breath as long as possible. *Oh, Breath of Heaven, why do I keep working to take in air?*

At the foot of your cross, the soldiers bicker among themselves. They won't stay around until the end. It can take a long time for lawbreakers to die on a cross. Smoke from their fire spills like hot acid into your eyes when you open them. One of them says, "Hey, guys, we're in luck. There's a piece of clothing here for all four of us." "Oh, and look, his outer garment is remarkable. It has no seams, so you know it came from the same bundle of thread. Someone spent a lot of time crafting this. Here, feel it. It's smooth, yet it's strong." "Let's not cut it. Let's roll the dice and see who the gods choose to wear this fine robe."

You want to cry, to feel a stream of tears fall to earth and expel the hurt from within your bones. But crusting blood from the needle-sharp thorns gums your eyes. Hungry flies circle and wait their turn to feast on your torn flesh. Blood in your mouth curdles like old milk. Sunlight drains from the sky even though it's the middle of the day. It's cold.

The capacity within humanity to inflict such pain on its own kind stuns even the Son of Man.

Meanwhile, standing near the cross of Jesus were his mother, and his mother's sister, Mary the wife of Clopas, and Mary Magdalene. When Jesus saw his mother and the disciple whom he loved standing beside her, he said to his mother, "Woman, here is your son." Then he said to the disciple, "Here is your mother." And from that hour the disciple took her into his own home.

Startled by voices that touch the past, you force a sticky eyelid open and recognize a treasured face in the crowd, the first human face you trusted. She's here. She loves you with all her broken heart. A wave of peace sweeps briefly through your battered body, and the gasp you take is like the air on top of the mountain you love and cool spring water flows quickly through your burning veins.

Her eyes are frozen in a confounded glaze. *Dear woman! How could you have known this was my purpose for being born? Like others, you heard my predictions. I saw dread and heaviness flood into your heart each time. We always had so much fun when we were together. The light we found within the moments we were together always chased away the darkness. Yet this is more than any mother can bear. Can there be any grace for you in this moment?*

She comes near. Your trusted friend tenderly wraps his arm around her and draws her close. *Thank you, Father, for providing someone to help her through this agonizing time.* Her lips move, but there is no sound. You know the prayer she is praying. It was her favorite and echoes your own prayer. *Yea, though I walk through the valley of the shadow of death, I will fear no evil for you are with me.* . . .

Again you force your eyes open and see how deeply her heart is pierced. She opens her mouth, but only moans ascend from the hollow pit of her soul. No fire of hell could touch these depths. She grips John's arm as her knees buckle.

Your life has been one of healing, and you won't leave without planting a seed for her healing, for this faithful woman who many years ago said to the angel, *"I am the Lord's servant. May it be to me as you have said."* How faithfully she has served.

Summoning the courage to gulp another breath, and praying she understands your mumbling through parched lips, you say, "Woman, see! Your son." Gulping another breath, you cry, "See, your mother." She clutches John and his arms keep her from falling to the ground.

* * *

Given that the fullness of God was shown in Jesus, visualize the story again but this time replace the name *Jesus* with a name for God that helps you imagine the Father/Creator in his place. Names to insert might be *Love*, *Goodness*, *Creator*, the *Breath of Life*, or come up with your own. Let this new encounter enrich your understanding of the nature and character of the Creator God.

When you are finished, reflect on how imagining the Creator in Jesus's place influences your understanding of God.

*   *   *

*"I will cleanse them from all the guilt
of their sin against me,
and I will forgive all the guilt
of their sin and rebellion against me.
And this city shall be to me
a name of joy, a praise, and an honor
before all the nations of the earth
who shall hear of all the good
that I do for them;
they shall fear and tremble because of
all the good and all the prosperity
that I provide for it."*
Jeremiah 33:8-9

*   *   *

Story #29 Jesus's Death

Like a lamb, innocent and without crime, Jesus accepted the punishment inflicted upon him without retaliation. In this story, imagine you are a resident of Jerusalem, watching as Jesus suffers shame before the world and before the Creator he loves so much. Imagine the Creator turning away as if his own heart is breaking. Watch as the nails, the whips, the thorns that create openings in Jesus's flesh and drain his lifeblood. Imagine you are at the foot of the cross as this absorption of pain starts to bring incredible healing to the creation.

Take a moment to relax. Pray to be led by the Holy Spirit, and then enter into the story.

See – Listen – Taste – Smell – Touch

Matthew 27:45–56

From noon on, darkness came over the whole land until three in the afternoon. And about three o'clock Jesus cried with a loud voice, "Eli, Eli, lema sabachthani?" that is, "My God, my God, why have you forsaken me?"

You've been a merchant in the city of Jerusalem all your life. This has been a hard week of work, busy because of the Passover feast, and you need to take a walk to get away from the stress. A body can be pushed only so far and you have learned to listen to yours. As you find an opening in the two-way stream of bodies flowing through a gate in the wall surrounding the city, you see a crucifixion is in progress. You wondered why there were so many people on this path today. Why does this destruction of human life attract so many spectators? It's disgusting. *Who are the unlucky victims today? Is it anyone I know?*

Three bodies hang from crosses. One is a bloody mess, while the other two have no external wounds. The scene draws you toward it with a morbid attraction. So cold, the flogged one hangs naked. So humiliating. . . . Blood coats every part of him. His feet have nothing to brace against so that he can raise his body to breathe. Only the nails piercing his feet allow him to rise up when he straightens his battered body. Deep cuts and gashes cover his skin, his hands, his face—every inch is bruised, bloodied.

Something inside you tells you that you need to be here, with him. You don't even know him. Bright colored blood oozes through dried and thickened gashes. Life flows out of him. Some of the blood meanders down his thigh and drops to the dirt. Some dries on his skin. A woman behind you whispers to her friend, "That's the rabbi, Jesus of Nazareth." What? You know who this guy is, though only through stories and the hype of the scribes and Pharisees. But what did he do? How could they do this to such a kind and loving man? Why?

How odd. It's like the morning light has started to bleed out of the sky. It's noon and yet the light is gone. You can't move your feet. They seem rooted in front of this cross. For three hours, the light from a few torches and a small fire illuminates his face. Shadows from the soldiers' fire crawl the ground. This murderous hill has always felt dark. More so today.

Nothing about this makes sense to you. Wait, he speaks. In a raspy voice, he questions the presence of God. People said he was always so sure about his Father God. Where is that God now? That's why you've not paid much attention to that religious stuff. What good is it if it makes people do this to you? *If God would get him out of this one, maybe even I would believe.*

When some of the bystanders heard it, they said, "This man is calling for Elijah." At once one of them ran and got a sponge, filled it with sour wine, put it on a stick, and gave it to him to drink. But the others said, "Wait, let us see whether Elijah will come to save him."

Jesus speaks something in Aramaic. People standing nearby turn their heads. "Did he say 'Elijah'? Is he calling down the prophet for help to destroy all these unbelievers? Or is the pain causing him to hallucinate?"

"Wait, don't give him any painkiller; we want to see if this is where he calls down fire from heaven! He and miracle-working Elijah as his helper, ha!"

"Come on, Jesus, this is your last chance to make a dramatic display. Give us a story to tell our grandchildren."

Shaking your head, you turn away. *How can people be so crass? They talk like this is a children's game.*

Then Jesus cried again with a loud voice and breathed his last. At that moment the curtain of the temple was torn in two, from top to bottom. The earth shook, and the rocks were split. The tombs also were opened, and many bodies of the saints who had fallen asleep were raised. After his resurrection they came out of the tombs and entered the holy city and appeared to many.

A guttural sound erupts from Jesus's torso and people in the distance turn to look at him.

You know that death from these crucifixions can be a long process, sometimes taking up to two days. *This man's got too much time left. No one who is near to death can cry out that loudly.* You've got to get back to your work. Your feet loosen their grip on the earth, and you take a step backward to walk away.

But a woman nearby gasps and says, "Look! He's not breathing. He stopped breathing."

You look up and see that it's true. He hangs limp, strangely serene.

Like a thousand pages of law tearing in two, the curtain of the temple that once separated people from the knowledge of God rips wide open.

The foundation beneath the holy city and the area surrounding Jerusalem rumbles and jerks. "This is the end!" a spectator shrieks as he scrambles to reach a path leading down the hill. You look at Jerusalem to see several tall buildings crumble and fall. People scream, "Everything is falling apart! We're going to die!" They scatter like frightened sheep.

You grab the first solid thing you can find to secure yourself and wrap your arms around it until the ground stops quaking. Opening your eyes, you slowly release your grip. In the darkness, you notice blood on your hands, and on your chest, and on your cheek. Instinctively, you push away. *It's his cross!* Grabbing a rag on the ground, you try to rub the blood from your clothes and skin.

Now when the centurion and those with him, who were keeping watch over Jesus, saw the earthquake and what took place, they were terrified and said, "Truly this man was God's Son!"

The officer of the Roman army who supervised the orders to nail Jesus to the cross gets to his feet and brushes the dirt from his knees and forearms. He pushes you aside and looks up at the lifeless body on the cross. Talking to no one in particular, he says, "The sun goes out in the middle of the day when we nailed this man to his cross. He hangs for only three or four hours. Then he dies suddenly. No one dies this quickly on the cross. That's what torture is about, slow death. The gods were merciful to this man. Then, when he dies, the earth groans and shakes—this one truly was the son of God."

Many women were also there, looking on from a distance; they had followed Jesus from Galilee and had provided for him. Among them were Mary Magdalene, and Mary the mother of James and Joseph, and the mother of the sons of Zebedee.

When you turn to walk back to the city, you notice a surprising number of women standing in the distance. *Why didn't I notice them earlier? There are so many.* They weep quietly and pull their head coverings over their faces whenever a temple guard or priest walks by. No other civilians remain.

As you walk the path toward the city, the sun breaks through the darkness and light spreads over the land. A weight seems to lift from the earth. *Something new is happening here.*

* * *

Given that the fullness of God was shown in Jesus, visualize the story again but this time replace the name *Jesus* with a name for God that helps you imagine the Father/Creator in his place. Names to insert might be *Love, Goodness, Creator*, the *Breath of Life*, or come up with your own. Let this new encounter enrich your understanding of the nature and character of the Creator God.

When you are finished, reflect on how imagining the Creator in Jesus's place influences your understanding of God.

O TASTE AND SEE

* * *

Through him
you have come to trust in God,
who raised him from the dead
and gave him glory,
so that your faith and hope
are set on God.
1 Peter 1:21

* * *

Story #30   The Walk to Emmaus

Two followers of Jesus have unbelievable news to tell their families and friends. Bad news. . .and strange news. They will meet Jesus and walk with him for several miles without recognizing him. The news the women brought from the tomb that morning was so unbelievable—so unimaginable. They're not sure if they can believe he's really alive. They are confused. Imagine yourself as one of these men, walking briskly to Emmaus to tell others what has happened.

Take a moment to relax. Pray to be led by the Holy Spirit, and then enter into the story.

See – Listen – Taste – Smell – Touch

Luke 24:13–35

Now on that same day two of them were going to a village called Emmaus, about seven miles from Jerusalem, and talking with each other about all these things that had happened. While they were talking and discussing, Jesus himself came near and went with them, but their eyes were kept from recognizing him.

Stepping to the side, you let a man pulling his wooden cart have the right of way. Rocks on the narrow road cause his cargo of woven baskets to bounce and nearly spill onto the ground. You step quickly to level ground as your companion, Cleopas, jabbers like a nervous teenager. You were chosen to bring an important message to your hometown, but you don't know how you're going to explain what happened. Nothing like this has ever happened. Jesus of Nazareth, your teacher and healer, was crucified, then buried in Joseph's tomb. The last two days remain a blur. And now, the women who went to tend to his body say the tomb is empty. Surely they must have been hallucinating. Yet Simon Peter also saw Jesus wasn't in the tomb. What can happen next?

"Look what I've done, Cleopas—I left my tools in Jerusalem, and I forgot to drop the money off to pay my taxes. I'm not thinking clearly today. All I can think about is that the Teacher is gone."

Another path converges with the one you walk. A man stands waiting for you to pass by. "Hello, stranger. We're going to Emmaus with some news. Feel free to join us as we walk."

And he said to them, "What are you discussing with each other while you walk along?" They stood still, looking sad. Then one of them, whose name was Cleopas, answered him, "Are you the only stranger in Jerusalem who does not know the things that have taken place there in these days?" He asked them, "What things?" They replied, "The things about Jesus of Nazareth, who was a prophet mighty in deed and word before God and all the people, and how our chief priests and leaders handed him over to be condemned to death and crucified him. But we had hoped that he was the one to redeem Israel. Yes, and besides all this, it is now the third day since these things took place. Moreover, some women of our group astounded us. They were at the tomb early this morning, and when they did not find his body there, they came back and told us that they had indeed seen a vision of angels who said that he was alive. Some of those who were with us went to the tomb and found it just as the women had said; but they did not see him."

"Yes, I'd like to join you. What's happening?"

The road converging with yours also leads out of Jerusalem. "Where have you been? Everyone in Jerusalem is talking about this," Cleopas says. "We're talking about Jesus of Nazareth, the teacher we were following. We were sure he was the promised Messiah who was going to lead Israel out of bondage to those godless Romans. Even though we weren't part of the inner group of disciples, we were hopeful of helping his rise to glory."

Cleopas pauses to catch a breath, so you add, "The bad news is that they killed him, crucified him like a common criminal."

"Yet strange things are happening now," he exclaims.

You step aside for a donkey pulling another cart full of fresh wool sheared that morning. You go on, "This is the third day since that happened, and the tomb where they laid him was found empty this morning. The women who tended to him saw angels; they said Jesus was alive! We thought that was impossible, especially after seeing his dead body lowered from the cross."

Cleopas adds, "Where have you been? On a mountain somewhere? This experience has really been brutal for us."

Then he said to them, "Oh, how foolish you are, and how slow of heart to believe all that the prophets have declared! Was it not necessary that the Messiah should suffer these things and then enter into his glory?" Then beginning with Moses and all the prophets, he interpreted to them the things about himself in all the scriptures.

As the man speaks, his words are like rain on dry, crusty ground as they sink into your heart. How does he know so much? "Do you not remember the prophecy in the writings of Genesis that *the scepter will not depart from Judah* until the Messiah comes?[9] Herod is not of Judah. And also, Isaiah announced *the Child will be called Wonderful, Counselor, Mighty God, Everlasting Father, Prince of Peace.*"[10]

This stranger knows the Scriptures incredibly well. Who has he studied under? How does he know what Moses and the prophets wrote and that it relates to Jesus? Again he says, "According to the prophet Isaiah, *'On this mountain...he will swallow up death forever'.*[11] And, *"He was despised and rejected by men...pierced for our transgressions...crushed for our iniquities...by his wounds we are healed. . . . He was led like a lamb to the slaughter. . . .so he did not open his mouth'.*"[12]

Your breathing is rapid and your eyes are open wide. *This is making so much sense.* "I never thought of things that way. Tell us more." Hearing these things makes you feel like you could walk another seven miles. It's almost like you've met this man before, maybe in a synagogue somewhere?

As they came near the village to which they were going, he walked ahead as if he were going on. But they urged him strongly, saying, "Stay with us, because it is almost evening and the day is now nearly over." So he went in to stay with them. When he was at the table with them, he took bread, blessed and broke it, and gave it to them. Then their eyes were opened, and they recognized him; and he vanished from their sight.

"Cleopas, look. We're entering Emmaus already. Where did the time go? This journey passed so quickly!" The sun sinks like a feather and touches the horizon. The man lifts his hand in a parting gesture. "No, no, friend. Don't go. We want to hear more. Stay with us and eat. We know a nice little place to grab some dinner. Join us, please."

With a smile, he consents.

The smell of freshly baked bread greets you as you step through the doorway. Cleopas exclaims, "I've not eaten a good meal since Friday morning. I'm famished. I'm sure I could eat a camel!" Finding a place to sit, you ask him, "Please, sir, say a blessing as we prepare to eat." Folding your hands, you bow your head. He prays. As he finishes praying, you lift your eyes to watch him break the bread. He offers it to you, and you reach out your hand. He places it gently into your open palm, and you look into his eyes. There's something so familiar. . . .

"Jesus! Cleopas, it's Jesus!" You turn your head to make sure Cleopas is paying attention. His eyes are as wide as your own and you hug each other. Then you turn to Jesus.

"What? Where is he? Oh, my Lord and my God! Where did he go? He is alive!"

They said to each other, "Were not our hearts burning within us while he was talking to us on the road, while he was opening the scriptures to us?" That same hour they got up and returned to Jerusalem; and they found the eleven and their companions gathered together. They were saying, "The Lord has risen indeed, and he has appeared to Simon!" Then they told what had happened on the road, and how he had been made known to them in the breaking of the bread.

"Honest, friends! We spoke with him for over an hour! We were not hallucinating. The Scriptures have been foretelling a different kind of Savior, one that's not about military or political power. We're not sure what it all means yet, but we recognized him when the bread was broken for us."

* * *

Given that the fullness of God was shown in Jesus, visualize the story again but this time replace the name *Jesus* with a name for God that helps you imagine the Father/Creator in his place. Names to insert might be *Love*, *Goodness*, *Creator*, the *Breath of Life*, or come up with your own. Let this new encounter enrich your understanding of the nature and character of the Creator God.

When you are finished, reflect on how imagining the Creator in Jesus's place influences your understanding of God.

End Notes:

[1] Unless otherwise noted, all Scripture quotations were taken from the New Revised Standard Version.

[2] A variation of its meaning is found in other places in the Gospel of John. In John 5:40; 6:35, 37, 44, 45, 65 the verb is credited by Thayer's Lexicon as meaning "to commit one's self to the instruction of Jesus and enter into fellowship with him." In John 3:20, it is credited as "to submit one's self to the power of the light." Used as a metaphor, the Greek word can mean "to show oneself," "to come into being," or "to find influence."

[3] Richard Rohr, *Things Hidden: Scripture as Spirituality* (Cincinnati, OH: St. Anthony Messenger Press, 2008), 127.

[4] Neil Douglas-Klotz, *Prayers of the Cosmos: Reflections on the Original Meaning of Jesus's Words* (HarperOne, 1993).

[5] Hal Zina Bennett, *Write from the Heart: Unleashing the Power of Your Creativity* (Novato, CA: Nataraj Publishing, 2001) 90.

[6] http://www.jewishencyclopedia.com/articles/865-adultery

[7] John 12:1-2 is another version of this story, identifying the woman as Mary, sister of Lazarus.

[8] Luke 10:38-42 has a story about two sisters, Mary and Martha, similar to John 12:1-2 that gives some reason to think this may be the same person.

[9] Genesis 49:10.

[10] Isaiah 9:6.

[11] Isaiah 25:7–8.

[12] Isaiah 53:3, 5, 7.

*　　*　　*

May the Prince of Peace,
the Spirit of Peace,
and the God of Peace
grow within you
as you love the Lord your God
with all your heart,
and with all your mind,
and with all your soul.

God is good. . .all the time.

*　　*　　*

About the author:

Paul W. Meier received a Masters of Divinity degree from Vanderbilt Divinity School and a Masters of Sacred Theology from Lutheran Theological Southern Seminary. He is a second career Lutheran pastor who has been published in The Upper Room, Christ In Our Home, Alive Now, The Lutheran, and Lutheran Partners. His other books include *Praying the Gospels with Martin Luther: Finding Freedom in Love*, *In Living Color: The Lord's Prayer*, and *In Living Color: The Beatitudes*.

Other books
by Paul W. Meier

Praying the Gospels with Martin Luther: Finding Freedom in Love

In Living Color: The Lord's Prayer

In Living Color: The Beatitudes

http://www.prayingthegospels.com/books

Made in the USA
Lexington, KY
02 January 2018